The Boy in England

Women
Singular Encounters
Of a Certain Age
More of a Certain Age
Speaking for the Oldie
A Timeless Passion
Tara and Claire
Asking Questions
In Conversation with
Insights
A Woman a Week
Dialogues
The Old Ladies of Nazareth

The Boy in England

NAIM ATTALLAH

QUARTET BOOKS

First published in 2005 by
Quartet Books Limited
A member of the Namara Group
27 Goodge Street
London W1P 2LD

A catalogue record for this book
is available from the British Library

ISBN 07043 71170

Typeset by Antony Gray
Printed and bound in Great Britain by
Creative Print and Design

Preface

After establishing the persona of 'the boy' in *The Old Ladies of Nazareth*, the first volume in this sequence of memoirs, writing about his early life in England turned out to be a most daunting task. I never kept a diary and had to rely mostly on memory. Despite this initial drawback, my recollection of events gathered momentum as I began the project. I also had recourse to friends from that era, with whom I had remained in close touch throughout the years.

I have tried notwithstanding to tell the story scrupulously of those ten years as they happened. There are no embellishments of the facts or exaggerations of incidents and their related circumstances. A recent fad in writing suggests it is common and acceptable to distort the truth for the sake of dramatization and good copy. I do not happen to agree. 'Creative licence' is also often used as an excuse to blur distinctions at the expense of honesty. The technique belongs to novels not to biography. Introducing such an element into my story of the boy would have been to undermine the integrity of the endeavour: to record the most formative period of his life when he endured sufferings and joy in equal measure.

The boy's personality and character were moulded into shape in that crucial time. He was fortunate to have had such diverse experiences, harsh as some of them may have been. They were responsible for contributing greatly to his evolution into a man who has no serious regrets to blight his life. However, if, in the course of setting out to tell his story, I have unwittingly caused offence to any with different views or with more rigid standards of morality, then I unreservedly offer my apologies. The only defence is that when truthfulness prevails it is worth the outcry that follows in its wake. It takes more courage to express the truth than to conceal it. I have in some cases refrained from naming people for their own protection, since I have no right to encroach on their privacy. I have also changed a number of individual names for the same reason.

In the summer of 2004 an unexpected turn of events caused me great disappointment. Its redeeming aftermath has been the motivating factor behind the writing of my memoirs. *The Old Ladies of Nazareth*, already published, was the prelude. *The Boy in England* will now be followed by two further volumes. Nature has its own way of redressing the balance. Something precious is awakened when adversity strikes. In my own case, I have come to feel that, in the autumn of a long, eventful life, I still have a great deal to contribute before the final curtain descends.

NAIM ATTALLAH

Acknowledgements

I would like to pay tribute to my wife Maria for jogging my memory and for reading each section of the book as I wrote it. Her encouragement was the defining factor in the expeditious completion of the manuscript.

My friend Adam Rudzki reminded me of many events I had forgotten, and so did Julie and Johnny Garnett. To them I owe my most sincere thanks. And last but not least, I am grateful to my editor Peter Ford for his diligence, his eye for detail and his total professionalism.

A Flower in the Morning

O flower of dawning,
O flower of the sky,
You pay your homage to God
With your ravishing beauty,
I see it all with my eye.
There is a sonorous music I can hear;
It comes from the murmured song of a nearby rill.
You enchant me with your playing in the wind,
As the clear blue sky entrances you as well.
The trees bend and sway about you
As you dip and bob against the rim of a hill.
Those showered in wealth could never have
As much contentment as you,
While those who are most blessed look on,
Consumed with envy too.

باب الشعر

الزهرة في الصباح   (نسيم عطا الله)

يا زهرة الصباح   يا عطية السماء.
ارانا تبين الله   في جمالك الضياء.
محولك الاشجار تتمايل   وانت تتلألئي في الفضاء.
اسمع حولك صوت جميل   وهو صوت خرير الماء.
فما اجملك ايتها الزهرة   وانت تلعبي في الهواء.
اراك مسرورة   في جمال الماء الزرقاء.
فانت اسعد الملائكة   متى من الاغنياء.
منظرك الجميل   يجعله اسعد السعداء.

[9]

The poem on the preceding pages was written in Arabic by the boy at about the age of eleven and found many years later preserved among his father's papers

It was early in October 1949. At that time, most travel was still by sea and land rather than by air. The Italian ship the boy boarded in Haifa was *en route* for Genoa. The voyage would take five days.

During the first two days at sea the boy cut a lonely, forlorn figure, often glimpsed tucked away in a corner of the deck, deep in thought and visibly apprehensive. He stared constantly at the calm waves of the eastern Mediterranean, and anyone who could have read his thoughts would have known how fearful he was, wondering what might become of him in a foreign land. At eighteen years of age he was hardly a boy any longer, but he had never travelled abroad before; nor had he travelled extensively in the Holy Land, where he had been born and raised. For that reason alone, the idea of travel was so alien to him as to trigger a deep-seated fear of a sort that remains dormant in most people. He was totally unprepared for the uncertainties of a journey that was taking him so far from his roots. For the first time in his life he was going to have to fend for himself, without the support of family or the many friends he was leaving behind. He had never felt so alone.

Genoa would not be the end of his journey. From there he would continue onwards to England. His knowledge of English was formal rather than idiomatic, and the matter of local habits and customs could raise some minor hurdles at the outset, though none of these, the boy assured himself, should cause him great difficulties. His mother tongue was Arabic, and he had been educated largely in French at a school run by monks; but English had also been taught as a secondary language, if not to the same level of fluency.

The image he had of the English was confusing to his young mind. He had known them mostly as a colonizing power, whose soldiers had a licence to deal roughly with the civilian Arab population. Memories were still vivid of British soldiers breaking down doors in the early hours of the morning, pushing and shouting at people as they rounded them up into lorries to be transported to large open spaces such as games arenas; there to have to endure the stifling heat of summer with no food or water for many long hours. The experience had left the boy mentally bruised and haunted. Even as a child he had been aware of the demeaning nature of the treatment. Could these soldiers have been the true representatives of their country in moral and ethical terms? He asked himself the question again and again. If they were, how could he hope to survive among such people? What chance would he stand of assimilating easily into his new environment?

Then another memory asserted itself. It was of being in Nazareth with his grandmother and great-aunt. At the far end of their garden was a pine tree under which he used to sit and read voraciously. He tackled any book he could lay hands on, whether it was in French or English. Under the pine he had read many classics of European literature, as well as such modern writers as Thomas Mann and Pearl S. Buck, the American author who wrote about life in China. The historical romances of Alexandre Dumas and Rafael Sabatini had absorbed his imagination, but he felt even more at home with the dramas of William Shake-speare – though Shakespeare sent him off to consult the dictionary more than most other writers. He loved George Bernard Shaw for the worldly humour of his insights and Oscar Wilde for the brilliance of his wit.

The English language itself was not something he had difficulty relating to. He felt impatient to reach a point where it came to him with ease and turned him into a competent writer. This had been the ambition he had harboured from a very young age. His dream of England was of a place of learning where he might one day establish himself and perhaps become well known in whatever field he had chosen. He desperately wanted to like England, to dispel any ill feeling that lingered as a result of the maltreatment received by his family, along with the rest of the Arab population, during the years of the British Mandate in Palestine. But the contrast between the splendour of the language and the brutality of the soldiers continued to create turmoil in his mind as he kept his lonely vigils on deck, making the first two days at sea hard to bear.

Then his feelings began to undergo a sea change: as he adapted himself to his situation so he awoke to the reality of his surroundings. His home in Haifa was receding into the realm of memory. The ship's deck on which he stood was his home for the present, till they docked in Genoa. He was reluctant to spend time below. The cabin had to be shared with two others and he felt the need to guard his privacy. At night it was another matter. After breathing in the strong sea air all day, he fell asleep the moment his head touched the pillow. Making friends did not come easily as yet; he had far too much on his mind to begin socializing. But all at once, and for no apparent reason, he decided he must pull himself together and start to circulate among his fellow passengers. He could see they were having some fun, and there seemed no reason why he should not join in.

Life has mysterious ways of changing direction. Suddenly it mends and transforms. The black clouds build up, the storm breaks, and blue skies return with renewed splendour. Nature is always at work, ravelling and unravelling. The boy was transformed by the realization. Life was for living; worry and apprehension were no longer on the agenda. The past must be left where it belonged and the future reached out for and grasped. His dreams must be made to come true. He would fulfil his long-held ambitions. The determination and fortitude of his grandmother and great-aunt would always be his guiding light.

The final three days of the voyage were spent like the other days on deck, but now they were passed in company with other young people. The fresh sea air doubled his appetite, as it did theirs. They were ravenous when mealtimes came round. Eating together provided the most pleasurable and memorable moments of the journey till they disembarked in Genoa and went their separate ways. The itinerary the boy's father had arranged for him with the agents Thomas Cook allowed him to spend a few hours in the town that was the birthplace of Christopher Columbus. At school in Haifa the boy had learnt how the inhabitants of Genoa were among the first Europeans to establish contact with the navigators of the Mediterranean – the Phoenicians and the Greeks. Charles

Dickens had spent time in the city in 1844 and loved it for the distinctive stone of its streets. Rubens, among other painters, had visited Genoa, and Anthony Van Dyck stayed there intermittently during the six years he worked in Italy; while there he painted the portraits of a number of grand Genoese aristocrats.

The boy, in the brief time he had for sightseeing, visited the famous early twelfth-century cathedral of St Lawrence, with its beautiful parti-coloured front dating in design from the transition point between the Romanesque and Gothic styles; and the chapel of St John the Baptist within the cathedral. Remains claimed to be the bones of John the Baptist as well as a glass plate said to be the very one on which Salome presented the head of the martyred saint to Herod were preserved in the cathedral. The boy marvelled at all he saw, and especially at the beauty and architectural splendour of this great maritime city of contrasts. He managed to see the famous cemetery, too; and could not resist going into a café to sample an authentic plate of pasta – which for him was the quintessential taste of Italy. Then it was time for him to head for the station to catch his train to Calais.

A totally exhausting journey out of Italy and across France followed. The train was jam-packed most of the way, and several hours went by before he was able to secure a seat. It came as a great relief to arrive at the docks and set foot on the gangplank of the ferry bound for Dover, though there were ominous predictions about the weather. It seemed the chances were it would take a turn for the worse as they made their crossing of the English Channel. The winds were already fairly strong as they waited in Calais. Nevertheless the captain took the decision to sail before conditions worsened.

Neither the boy nor any of the other travellers were able to relax for long once the ship got under way. As soon as they were out in the open sea the heavens unleashed a violent tempest. The winds, rising to storm force, stirred up the waters into mountainous waves that hurled themselves against the vessel. The boat was tossed about like a toy and the scene inside rapidly became one of devastation. Bottles of drink, glasses and crockery flew off the shelves and were smashed; chairs and tables were flung from one end of the passenger lounge to the other. The boy had never witnessed anything like it. Frightened passengers clung tightly to whatever remained securely bolted in place; children cried and people screamed.

The boy himself, who had always been frightened of the sea and had never learnt to swim, was terrified out of his wits. Could this be his destiny: to leave home and be lost at sea before he had a chance to arrive anywhere else? Such extremity of fear paralyses the body and freezes the brain; courage becomes difficult to muster. For fourteen hours the thunderous battering of the waves continued without remission. For much of that time the power of the engines was held in check, to reduce the impact of the waves on the body of the ship and help protect the passengers as it rode out the storm. The stench of people's vomit was caught and held in the nostrils for as long as the nightmare lasted.

All the passengers were looking pale and drawn as they disembarked at Dover, but inside they were feeling deliriously happy to be leaving the ordeal and misery behind. The boy, too, though visibly shaken, could breathe a fervent sigh of relief at having come through the worst experience of his young life. For the first time, he felt, he had stared death in the face and survived. It was something he was never going to be able to forget: seeing the sea in a merciless rage and his life hanging on the edge of extinction.

His journey on the Dover train to London was the quiet culmination of what had turned out to be an adventure more real and perilous than anything he could have imagined. He knew that his uncle on his mother's side, who had lived in England for several years, would be waiting to greet him at the terminal. The plan was for his uncle to take him to introduce him at an address in Oakley Gardens, Chelsea, where he himself rented a room. There the boy would lodge in the house of a charming middle-aged lady, who also looked after a blind man and his wife. The house would be his home for many months.

Oakley Gardens was a desirable street tucked away in the heart of Chelsea. It was close to Cheyne Walk and the Chelsea Embankment, and the King's Road lay to the north. There were many literary associations, and famous living writers of the day, such as Daphne du Maurier, had their home there. Not far away, over near Sloane Street, was the Cadogan Hotel, where Oscar Wilde had been arrested before his notorious trial.

The house where the boy's uncle took him had a comfortable look about it, and it proved indeed to be most welcoming. The landlady was Miss Eva Willmott. She was short of stature and had been born with a spinal deformity known in those days as a hunchback. She totally ignored this physical disability and got on with her life actively and contentedly. The blind man and his wife occupied the top floor, while a Scottish student, studying to become a vicar, lived below them on the first floor, adjacent to a room that Miss Willmott designated her own. The boy and his uncle had a room each on the ground floor, and the basement was used as a dining-room with a kitchen next to it. One other inhabitant of the house, and the one who took pride of place, was Cherie, Miss Willmott's cat. Cherie was rather plump, moderately furry, and considered the whole house to be her domain. The lives of cat and owner were closely intertwined. If Miss Willmott was in the house, Cherie rarely ventured outside, but when Miss Willmott was away at work during the day, she would sit out on the pavement awaiting her return. Instinctively she knew the hour when this would be, and would scamper off to greet her mistress before escorting her back to the front door.

Miss Willmott worked on a part-time basis as secretary to Frances Newton, a formidable personality who lived in a grandly sumptuous apartment in a prestigious block of flats off Sloane Square. Miss Newton was an Irish missionary who had worked in Palestine since long before the years of the British Mandate. She had cut a colourful figure in the Holy Land, habitually smoking cigars and riding about on a white horse during her travels. Among the Arabs she was a legend. Her main claim to fame stemmed from her eviction from Palestine by the British authorities for stirring up political trouble. She was a champion of the cause of an independent Palestine where Arabs and Jews could live side by side in harmony. A two-state solution was something with which she was in vehement disagreement. Her conviction remained that peace could only be attained if the Balfour Declaration was laid aside in favour of the creation of a single state. Her eviction from the Holy Land, accompanied by a total ban on her ever returning there, was sanctioned by the British government, who considered her a potential threat to the peace and stability of the region. In London she remained equally troublesome, dabbling in politics and concerning herself especially with the question of Palestine. She made her position clear when she published her autobiography and called it *Fifty Years in Palestine: The Case for the Arabs* (1948).

Miss Newton was born into a landowning family from whom she inherited her wealth. Her Irishness came to her through her mother, whose home was in County Waterford. Her father had a large manorial estate in Derbyshire, where she grew up under the tutelage of a half-Italian, half-German governess who helped to develop her aptitude for languages. The governess was chosen as a fit person to be in charge of the Newton children on account of the fact that she had come out of the Roman Catholic Church and converted to Protestantism. 'At home,' Miss Newton wrote, 'we were certainly brought up on Holy Writ.' Every day there were morning prayers for the household at 8 a.m., and after lunch bible-reading lessons for members of the family and any visitors who happened to be present. Though the children had ponies and horses to ride, they were forbidden to attend the local Quorn hunt. Playing cards was taboo and at parties they had to leave before the dancing began.

Despite her stern evangelical upbringing, Miss Newton's London apartment was a focus for social gatherings where the rich and famous intermingled. The distinction of being seen in the desirable surroundings of Miss Newton's *salon* was an honour widely sought. At teatime she met her lady friends for some animated gossip, as her companion, a sort of lady-in-waiting who administered everything on her behalf, saw that nothing went amiss. In the evenings she entertained political leaders and selected distinguished journalists, as well as others known to have influence in high places.

Miss Newton was a tall, well-built, rather handsome woman with striking features and conspicuous strength of character. During her childhood one of her greatest pleasures had been to escape the sharp eye of her governess to visit the forbidden area of the estate blacksmith's shop, known as 'Ikey's hole'. There she and her sisters learnt how to forge horseshoes out of iron. If Ikey spotted the governess on the horizon, he would hustle the girls into his back yard and give them a leg-up over the wall so they could escape across the churchyard to the manor-house garden without being detected. She was still in her teens when a stepsister, who worked for the Church Missionary Society in Jaffa, offered to take her back with her to Palestine. It was the start of a fifty-year association with the country she called her second homeland. Later, when she was on leave in Derbyshire, she persuaded a jeweller to show her how to dismantle and reassemble a clock.

Subsequently, she would collect treasured but broken-down clocks from villagers in Galilee in her saddlebags, bring them back to England and eventually restore them to their owners in working condition.

All these stories testified to the forcefulness of her personality. In her retirement in London she never minced her words and tended to become abrasive if anyone debated against her, especially if the Palestine question arose. It was an issue on which she was totally uncompromising, and she never flinched from the battle to put across her deep concerns about the precarious situation being created by the retreat of the British and the foundation of the new Israeli state. She truly loved Palestine with every fibre of her being. She felt that her spiritual home was there, among the peasants and the holy sites. If she possessed strong religious views, these were never on public display, and the general conclusion was that she was more interested in politics than religion, despite being a missionary.

Miss Willmott was somewhat bewildered by the high-powered environment created by Miss Newton, but equally she was fascinated by all the comings and goings at her place of work. Occasionally she would give way to an outburst of scorn at what she called the manly behaviour of her employer. Miss Newton was not one for womanly pursuits. 'I love and respect a good tool,' she wrote, 'but how I hate a needle!' Miss Willmott found her quite over-bearing in her eccentricities and often showed signs of irritation at the way she would light up a pipe and settle imperiously into a large comfortable armchair with a glass of whisky in one hand and a full bottle in convenient reach of the other. These indulgences in drink and tobacco were no doubt reactions against a childhood of extreme piety, but Miss Willmott was not prepared to make any allowances on that account. They were something of which she especially disapproved. As a devout Anglican, she was not in the least in sympathy with such excesses. To do charitable work was a central aim in her life and she was ever ready to help the needy and the infirm. There was a quality of goodness in her that the boy had rarely encountered in anyone before, and her generosity, bestowed out of limited means, was exemplary.

The boy struck up a warm friendship with Miss Willmott, who became his unofficial tutor. She helped him with his English lessons and often corrected his home-work. The boy had enrolled at a tutorial college in Tottenham Court Road, and there he spent the best part of the day before returning home at around 4 p.m. By that time Miss Willmott was usually already home as well, setting about organizing the evening meal for everyone in the house. Britain in 1949 still retained much of its system of rationing left over from the war. Many types of food were not readily available, especially meat, except for rabbit, which was plentiful and off the ration. Rabbit pie and casserole were therefore eaten in great quantities, though everyone seemed to enjoy whatever was put on the table. In those days selectivity of diet was not something even thought about. People lived simply and accepted a lack of choice as a matter of fact. They were happy with what was obtainable. Many basic commodities were hard to come by; luxuries that would come to be considered commonplace after the years of austerity were non-existent. The abundance of choice now taken for granted can have a downside, for people are often grateful to have their decisions made for them by circumstances.

With money in such short supply, the Londoners of 1949 had a struggle to maintain some sort of living standards. Unemployment was high and the economy was suffering a heavy burden from the after-effects of six years of war. The great city as a whole still showed all the signs of having been under heavy bombardment. Some of its finest buildings were pock-marked with the scars of shrapnel and there were gaps in many streets where houses had once stood. Some surviving buildings were shored up with heavy timber supports to keep them standing until they could be repaired. Other sites had been cleared for the construction of one-storey prefabricated houses, known as 'prefabs', as part of the London County Council's strategy to deal with the accommodation crisis and provide temporary homes for bombed-out families.

There was a constant feeling of melancholy in the air. The boy's imagination had to work hard to visualize how London had been before the war. Many elements from the past survived, but they seemed to have lost much of their character amid persisting dereliction and the beginnings of reconstruction in a city that looked like one large building site. The boy's first reaction was one of total bewilderment. He was unnerved by the London fog, especially when it developed into an all-obscuring yellow smog that left an acrid taste in the mouth and throat. The reasons for it were not hard to deduce. A majority of households still relied on open coal fires to keep themselves warm in winter, while across the River Thames from the Chelsea Embankment the tall landmark chimneys of Battersea Power Station fed columns of smoke into the atmosphere. To set against this, on a more positive note, some bomb-sites turned themselves into small nature reserves in the summer. A profusion of flowering plants like willowherb and buddleia attracted clouds of colourful butterflies.

The boy's friendship with Miss Willmott developed to the point where they derived comfort from each other's company. Although Miss Willmott was energetically occupied all day, she had no social friends to speak of. She looked after her lodgers with meticulous care, and the money she received from them was just enough to cover the household outgoings and leave her with a modest income. The rent she received from each of them was £2 10s. (£2.50) a week, which included food, laundry, electricity and heating. There was a telephone in the house, though it was rarely used. The disruption of universal serenity occasioned by the mobile-phone invasion was still decades away and people managed to get by perfectly well without the means of instant communication that was to become such an essential feature of twenty-first-century life.

In the evenings, after an early dinner, normally at 6 p.m., Miss Willmott and the boy would set off on long walks. Their favourite route took them along the Chelsea Embankment beside the River Thames, starting from Albert Bridge then turning north along Chelsea Bridge Road towards Sloane Square. At the square they turned west to go along the King's Road till they reached Chelsea Town Hall. From there it was a stone's throw back down Oakley Street to Oakley Gardens. All the way, keeping up a brisk pace, they engaged in deep conversation. The boy often gesticulated as he became excited about a point he was making, and Miss Willmott paid serious attention to everything he said. It was a relationship that defied the age gap and enriched them both. Miss Willmott was enchanted by the boy's enthusiasm and his optimism in general. For his part, he was delighted to discover an attentive, sympathetic listener who did not reject his opinions out of hand. A particularly wild idea or a misplaced judgement might earn a gentle rebuke from her, though she was always supportive. This supportiveness, which was almost unconditional, created more than a hint of jealousy among the other lodgers. Even the boy's uncle, who had regarded himself as quite close to Miss Willmott before the boy's arrival, started to show signs of resentment as their friendship developed.

As the boy settled securely into his new home, gone were the awful memories of the humiliations suffered at the hands of the British forces at the time of the Mandate by him, his family and their Palestinian neighbours. He was seeing a very different side of the British here in their own country. His impression so far was that the majority he met were kind and courteous and had impeccable manners. It was a relief to find that his apprehensions about the British could no longer be justified. He began to feel confident that he would have little difficulty assimilating into their way of life. The principles and ideals that had made Britain a great nation were something with which he could begin to identify.

His education, too, progressed better than expected. By the time he was only three months through his six-month course, he was already not far off completing the entire curriculum. At its completion he could sit his matriculation exams before applying for university entrance; and in fact the final three months went smoothly and he attained good grades in every subject. There was jubilation in Oakley Gardens. Miss Willmott cooked a special dinner for everybody in the house and baked a cake to mark the occasion. Not even Cherie was forgotten, but received a special treat so she should not feel aggrieved at being left out of the party.

The boy had his own mischievous relationship with the cat. He loved to tease her. When he had a leisure moment he would sit opposite her, dangling a gold chain with a medallion hanging on the end of it. This he would allow to swing like a pendulum, to see how long it took to induce hypnosis. At first the cat's eyes would dart from side to side as she tried to follow the movement of the medallion. After a few minutes, as if she were entranced by the exercise but utterly exhausted in the process, her eyes would close and she would fall into a deep slumber. One day Miss Willmott caught the boy carrying out his experiment. It was a rare occasion on which she became extremely angry with the boy and berated him for being cruel to her darling Cherie.

With his qualifications achieved, the boy managed to secure a place for himself at Battersea Polytechnic, today the University of Surrey, on the south side of the river. His uncle, who was eleven years older, was already studying there for a B.Sc. degree in mechanical engineering. The offer of the place, however, was conditional on his spending two full terms at the college's preparatory division before he could be enrolled as a student within the engineering faculty. He consented to this condition and thus began the scholastic life of the boy, a life to which he had looked forward for so long.

Growing up in Palestine with a highly protective father, the boy had never been taught to swim for fear he might drown. He had never been allowed to go on a picnic with other boys, because of the danger of his getting hurt. He was never even given a bicycle, in case trying to ride it led to a fall. The first thing the boy did, following his acceptance as a student at the Battersea Polytechnic, was buy himself a bicycle. The night before he went out to make his purchase he could hardly sleep from excitement. The bicycle, once he had bought it, became his pride and joy. Learning to ride it took him no time at all. He could now cycle to college without having to wait around for public transport. He had acquired the freedom of the entire metropolis, and he could commute at will, without the risk of being late for a lecture or an appointment. He had achieved his first objective and made the ownership of a bicycle a reality. There are those who see such small things as trivial, but for others they can be crucial to development in terms of boosting confidence. In the past, being given a handgun by a gun-running cousin in Nazareth had had the same effect. With the weapon in his possession he had felt confident and able to hold up his head among the crowds.

His first few days at the polytechnic's preparatory school were largely spent in making friends and getting acquainted with his new surroundings. The teachers, most of them men, were kind and helpful. The atmosphere in the school was congenial. Before long it became clear that he excelled in mathematics, and he was often congratulated by his tutor, who in due course strongly recommended he pursue a degree in mathematics.

The boy fitted in extremely well and attracted great popularity in a short time, partly because he was so full of mischief. He soon organized a small gang of students of whom he was the leader. The gang roamed about the school, claiming territorial rights and causing disruption; one woman teacher who was bereft of any sense of humour was less than amused. The boy found himself summoned by the college principal, Dr Waring. Dr Waring refused to over-dramatize the affair, and justified it to the woman teacher on the grounds that boys must sometimes give vent to their frustrations if they were eventually to grow into responsible members of society.

Dr Waring was a man in his early fifties, of medium build and height. He was softly spoken and rarely raised his voice in anger. Nevertheless he conveyed authority and inspired respect in ways commensurate with his position. His good looks gave him an added cachet. Girl students would whisper to each other in admiration as they passed him in a corridor. He was noted for the breadth of his knowledge and all who knew him considered him highly intelligent. Nothing escaped the notice of his sharp and searching eyes and he could display toughness and understanding in equal measure. He may well have been gay; he was certainly a highly popular figure, not only among the students but also with his contemporaries in the teaching profession. In his liberal views, as well as in his general response to every situation, he was a man ahead of his time.

It was obvious that Dr Waring had a soft spot for the boy, and though he rebuked him, he did so with a tolerant smile on his face. The boy got the message instantly. He was being favoured and sheltered by the principal (an enviable state of affairs he enjoyed throughout his whole period at the Battersea Polytechnic). From that day on, he brazenly broke college rules and controlled his gang by inflicting various punishments on any member who challenged his authority or refused to toe the line when asked to do so. Non-adherence to gang loyalty would result in the unhappy individual being tied to a chair and left unattended for several hours in an empty classroom. The more his leadership became unassailable and his stature grew among the students, the more rumbustious he became.

Any new student was obliged to undergo an initiation ceremony during which he or she would be tossed up into the air for two or three minutes in one of the thick blankets provided in every classroom for fire safety. When it came to the turn of a pretty girl to suffer the ritual, there would be a rumpus among the boys as to who would get to take up the privileged position from where there was a good chance of catching a glimpse of the girl's knickers – or lack of them. This matter was usually settled by the flick of a coin. All this must sound horrendous to modern ears, but their pranks were all undertaken in a good spirit and generated a great deal of fun. The participants in the initiation ceremony, including the so-called victims, seemed to enjoy every minute of it without exception.

The sudden rise of the boy in student society earned him influence in every area of college life. When it came to the union elections, any candidate who received his endorsement was sure to poll a majority. With his gang, he devoted time and effort to developing means of persuasion, some less reputable than others, to ensure his favourite candidate got the necessary student vote.

Table tennis had been the only sport the boy ever indulged in back home in Palestine. He had shown talent and flair for the game from a very early age and had been encouraged to practise every other day at least. In the polytechnic main building there was a large table-tennis room for the use of students during lecture breaks. Here he became a frequent visitor, and his talent for the game was soon a talking point. He was invited to coach as well as play in the team. Before long he found himself the recipient of many trophies. This led him to form a ladies' team. He then spent many happy hours in their company, teaching them the finer points. It brought him other, different rewards as he became the centre of their attention and revelled in this new sphere of activity.

On the social side, he had many friends, and there were five close friends in particular with whom he discovered common ground. Most weekends he would be invited down to the country to meet the parents and family of whoever had issued the invitation. A weekend in Surrey that came about as the result of one such invitation left an indelible impression. His friend's parents were what might today be called working middle class. They had over the years acquired a certain social status, not on the exalted level of stockbrokers or merchant bankers, but more in line with the professional occupations. They had learnt social etiquette as they left their working-class roots behind and climbed the ladder of success. Yet they still retained the no-nonsense philosophy of life of working people. While outgrowing their humble beginnings, they remained true to their origins in the sense that they were not ashamed to perform any menial task in the home rather than leave it for the daily help to do for them. There were certain things that they believed to be a man's personal responsibility, such as taking care of his family's shoes and seeing that they were clean; their concern even extended to the shoes of their guests.

The weekend in question was a rainy one. The boy and his friend came back from a walk with their shoes muddy and much in need of a clean and polish. The friend's father suggested they deposit their muddy footwear in the hall and produced slippers for them to wear about the house. In the morning, when the boy came downstairs to reclaim his shoes, he found the father had cleaned all the shoes himself and made sure they were given an excellent polish. It was something that impressed the boy deeply. Back home, and in the Middle East in general, it would have been improper for the head of a household to embark on such a task. As a general principle, shoes were items for servants to deal with. He was learning more about the British way of life and its unpretentious attitude to most things. It was this that seemed to make the British special.

At Oakley Gardens, life went on as usual, with Miss Willmott always preparing dinner at the same hour. Sometimes the food contained a small tuft of cat's fur, which had found its way into the dish of the day by some freak accident. Whenever this happened, Miss Willmott would apologize profusely, blaming the cat for this unfortunate intrusion into her culinary endeavours. When all was said and done, however, Miss Willmott's sense of hygiene was not among her strongest points. There was constantly a lingering fishy smell about the house, and all you could do was get used to it. It was no use mentioning it. Miss Willmott was extremely touchy on the subject, for she considered Cherie to be an integral part of her own existence. Thus anything that put into question the cat's desirability was a taboo subject. Such were the circumstances, and in the end the lodgers settled for a tactical truce with Cherie. It made life easier for all concerned.

One bright day, Miss Willmott decided that the time had come for the boy to meet the formidable Miss Newton. For this awesome encounter, he needed to be clean, smart and well groomed. The splendid apartment residence in which Miss Newton lived and worked was breathtaking. The trappings of wealth were everywhere in abundance. Beautiful antique carpets covered the floors; large oil paintings, mainly from the school of orientalism, hung on the walls; among the exquisite pieces of furniture, magnificent silver objects were polished to a flawless shine. A diffuse and gentle aroma of some incense was suspended in the air and had a soothing effect on the senses. White flowers were discreetly placed to add a finishing touch to this palatial establishment.

Miss Newton was large and overpowering in every sense. Her femininity was undoubtedly overshadowed by certain masculine traits, yet her charisma was all consuming. The boy sat in awe as she ordered tea and gestured to her lady companion to fill her three pipes with tobacco in readiness for the evening and place them, when full, on a small table next to her. A bottle of whisky also stood within reach. As they started tea, Miss Newton began to reminisce about her time in Palestine and how much she adored the peasants, who would invariably come out to greet her at the entrance to any village she happened to visit. She always arrived riding her white horse, as if it were her emblem. Anywhere in the Holy Land, if you mentioned the big Irish lady on the white horse, it was known that you were referring to Miss Newton.

She made the boy pile his plate high with sandwiches and cakes, and when the plate was empty, insisted he take more. It was a hospitable convention she must have picked up from the natives of Palestine, among whom the amount of food eaten by a visitor denotes both the generosity of the host and the appreciation of the guest. Generosity came naturally to Miss Newton; when it was time for the departure of the boy with Miss Willmott after tea, she discreetly pressed on him what was a substantial sum of money for those days. This, she explained, would buy him a smart suit for formal occasions and a woollen jumper to keep him warm when cycling to college in the winter. He mustn't think the gesture was because he gave an impression of being poorly dressed, she hurriedly assured him, but because she felt an impulse to indulge him.

In time the boy became a regular visitor of Miss Newton's, and was always greeted warmly. She never once failed to shower him with money, food and gifts. When he tried to curb her enthusiasm and suggest her kindness was all too much, she would have none of it. She insisted that it gave her immense satisfaction and pleasure, as well as a feeling of catharsis, to have an opportunity to compensate for the ill-treatment the Palestinians received from the British under the Mandate. Here he was, far from home in a foreign environment, and it was her wish to show him this hospitality to make up for any hurt he might have experienced earlier in his life. It should simply be seen as a gesture of good will, with overtones of national redemption.

Miss Newton was the sort of larger-than-life character one expects to encounter only in fiction. The boy felt that her entrance into his life was a sign of good omen; that the stars were surely moving in his favour. Whether his optimism was well founded only time would tell. The road ahead for most of us proves to be more testing than we ever imagine it will be.

Time passed quickly. At Battersea Polytechnic the boy was now fully integrated into the engineering faculty in main building. With his preparatory course finished, he was starting to prepare for his intermediate science course. It was the spring of 1951, the year of the Festival of Britain, and Miss Willmott's lease on the house in Oakley Gardens had about ten years left to run. Nevertheless she was preparing to dispose of it. During the years before the Second World War she had always lived in Streatham, and she longed to return to the familiarity of this south London borough. Her lodgers were therefore going to have to look for new accommodation. Streatham would be too far out for them, and Miss Willmott was looking for a different sort of property in any case. She was starting to feel the strain of looking after lodgers on top of her other commitments, chief among these being the blind man and his wife. The elderly couple were like family to her. They would always be her first priority, and she would keep them with her wherever she made her home.

The boy faced the prospect of moving house in his uncle's company with misgivings. The two of them were like chalk and cheese and there were bound to be problems. The only thing they had in common were family ties, and even these were the subject of niggling tensions. Although his uncle had been quite bright in his youth, most of the sparkle seemed to have been lost by the time he was thirty. Every line of his uncle's body and rounded face were already marked with disappointment. There was a slowness in the way he moved, and in his capacity to recollect and absorb things. As he was also rather inarticulate, he would jot down notes before visiting a friend or acquaintance to try and make sure he would be able to have a proper discourse with them. His extreme shyness made him tongue-tied in the presence of women, and often when he struggled to start a conversation, a clumsy awkwardness would spoil the attempt. So set was he in his ways that any deviation from a normal routine created major problems for him. He was deeply religious and attended mass regularly. He was obsessively careful with money and always strove to gain a bargain. On the positive side, it meant his life was well organized, but any idea of adventure went entirely against the grain. He hesitated over every decision and hated flippancy.

By contrast, all the boy's instincts were for spontaneity in thought and action. Their incompatibility did not bode well for life in the small house in Munster Road, Parsons Green, that the uncle found for them to rent. The departure from Oakley Gardens took place a few weeks after Miss Willmott declared her intention to move. The parting was emotional, though the boy realized that, much as he was attached to Miss Willmott, the time had come for a change. Whatever difficulties sharing a flat with his uncle might create, he was not yet ready to live on his own. He could only accept the situation with philosophical resignation. It was simply an inevitable but purely temporary measure, till the stars moved on and dictated change.

That summer an opportunity of easing these domestic constraints presented itself when a priest from the Holy Land arrived with a small cache of sovereigns sent by the boy's father. Almost two years had gone by since he had last seen his parents and grandmother, and the proceeds from the sale of the gold coins would be enough to finance a journey home. During the summer break from the poly-technic he therefore found himself retracing the train and ferry journey back to Genoa and boarding an Italian ship bound for Haifa.

He was allocated a bunk in the two-berth cabin he was to share with a handsome French youth who was very warm and friendly, full of Gallic panache and oozing charm. The boy was delighted to come across such an easy-going travelling companion. There was every sign it was going to make the journey a pleasant one. Having got themselves installed in their cabin, the Two Musketeers, as they subsequently came to be known, went on deck to familiarize themselves with the layout of the ship and begin scouting for any unattached girls who might also be on board. The French companion soon turned out to be a real ladies' man. He also had a way of inciting those in his company to get up to things they would never normally have dreamt of doing. His corrupting influence was irresistible.

A large contingent of Australian girls on their way to Israel to work on a kibbutz seemed heaven-sent. The French youth lost no time in infiltrating the group and sizing up the possibilities with a practised eye, seeking to ensure that he and the boy would have no shortage of female company throughout the voyage. The tactic was to play cards with the girls during the day, leading up to a game of strip poker if a corner could be found out of sight of other passengers and the crew. It was something the girls found highly amusing and entertaining. The boys could hardly believe their luck. At night the real fun began when the boys left their cabin and headed for a secluded part of the deck they had discovered, each carrying a woollen blanket to a prearranged rendezvous. Invariably two of the girls would appear and the four of them would tuck themselves away under the blankets to cuddle, kiss and make love to their hearts' content. The only rules were that no inhibitions were to be tolerated and it was both expected and desirable to swap partners. Such unimaginable pleasures were a revelation to the boy, who was still in the process of emerging from his youthful innocence. The exercise was repeated four nights running, always with different pairs of girls, until, a day out from Haifa, the boy met an English girl called Lara.

At Haifa harbour the French Lothario departed from the boy's life as swiftly as he had entered it. The boy was never to meet him again, though he often wondered what it would be like to run into him and see whether the camaraderie they had known aboard ship had survived the passage of time, or whether it would prove to have been as fleeting as the encounters under the blankets. The girl Lara was another matter. He could sense the beginning of a close relationship. She was travelling with her sister, and they were both on their way to work on a kibbutz. They came from a Jewish family in Cambridge. Before the passengers went ashore, he had made an arrangement to meet Lara again a week later.

Haifa as a town was little changed since he was last there, except that there were now Jewish families living in areas once inhabited by Arabs. The biggest changes were in the lives of his parents. Among the very few friends they had, most had either departed or were dead. The Arab population had certainly decreased, and there was an air of despondency among those who stayed. The future looked bleak, with no sign of better times ahead. Opportunities for young Arabs were scarce and racial tensions crushed any hope of harmonious coexistence between Arab and

Jew. The boy had a sense that he was skimming the surface, making a sentimental journey that lacked depth. He was in his home town, but had lost his bearings. He began to question whether his attachment to his roots, to the land of his birth, was as strong as it had been in the past, whether the passion to claim it as his own despite the occupation still burned in his heart.

There were many parts of the Holy Land he had never visited. When he went to meet Lara and her sister, they often set off on journeys of discovery together and were deeply impressed by what they saw, realizing that the biblical land of Palestine retained the power to enrich the spirit in so many ways. The aura of ancient times was all-pervasive, here in this place that was the cradle of Christianity. The land was revered by Jews, Christians and Moslems alike, and for this very reason evoked strong rivalries that led to strife and bloodshed. Its soil had been fought over again and again over two millennia, the irony being that these conflicts were always in the name of religion and peace.

As Lara and the boy became more romantically entangled, Lara's sister became increasingly disgruntled. She did not approve of the liaison. At times it was distinctly embarrassing, but in the end she was won over and the three of them became friends together. The sister developed the discreet habit of allowing the boy and Lara a measure of privacy on the occasions when passion needed to be quenched. When for one night they visited the house of the boy's grandmother in Nazareth, the three of them slept on a mattress on the floor of the main room, huddled together in total amity. The next morning, before they left to return to Haifa, Lara, who was planning to become a professional photographer, took pictures of the boy sitting with his grandmother and great-aunt in the garden. The photographs taken that day meant that his memory of the precious moment could be preserved and never become blurred with time.

For the boy it was a harshly poignant leave-taking. He knew he would probably never see the old ladies alive again. Until then, he had been struggling to resolve the dilemma of his loyalties; but now he had found the house of his earlier boyhood still as he remembered it. It was suffused with memories of such intensity that he realized they could not be taken from him or abandoned. This was indeed the soil in which he had his roots. He would never forsake or deny it. The legacy was set for ever in his mind and spirit.

Returned to Haifa, he spent the next few nights with Lara on Mount Carmel, in a public garden overlooking the bay, making the most of what time remained to them before she was due back in Cambridge. He felt a sadness that she would be leaving. He was certainly going to miss her. They got on so well together and had gained a deep comfort from each other's company. The stillness of the nights on the summit of the mountain and the panoramic view seemed to provide just the right setting for their fast-approaching emotional farewell. Although his own departure would be only a few days later, he knew the gap left by Lara must have an affect on him. Despite the fact of his roots, rediscovered in Nazareth, he was unable to see himself as anything except a stranger here – a visitor to the land of his birth. It was a struggle to relate to what was happening in the town where he had grown up and gone to school and from which he had once observed the world with a different pair of eyes. He felt like a fish out of water: no great distance from the sea yet stranded helplessly on the beach. The period of nostalgia associated with his journey was drawing to a definitive close.

The days after Lara's departure were devoted to visiting with his parents those few friends who remained, or seeking out antique shops in the company of his father. Occasionally he went shopping for fruit and vegetables, which was something he enjoyed, or else strolled through the German quarter, hoping to find corners he remembered from when they lived in their house in Mountain Road. There was little to do otherwise. He never went to the beach as he still could not swim. He only visited the cinema twice and could not say why it held no appeal for him, despite the fact that he was usually a keen moviegoer. It was as if the world of cinema could contribute nothing to the dramatic backdrop of his homecoming. He much preferred to sit around in the house, looking through his old possessions or reading some of the books he had left behind, rousing himself only when one of the stream of visitors who called to celebrate his return and pay their respects to his parents demanded his attention.

After lunch each day he retired to the small bedroom that he used to occupy and dreamed of the many hours he had spent there engrossed in his writing. Those were the days during the Second World War when without any outside help he produced a weekly paper, acting as editor, reporter and commentator. It was written in Arabic and contained current news about the war as well as a short story and a quiz to liven matters up. The paper was distributed among a select readership made up of family friends and received much praise for the quality of its writing and the originality of its content. It was impossible to say whether the praise was truly deserved or simply intended as a sign of encouragement. Either way the boy was grateful that his efforts were not going unnoticed, and a swagger in his step told it all. He looked back on those early stirrings of his journalistic ambitions with a mixture of pride and nostalgia. They had signalled the beginning of a lifelong love affair with the written word.

During his final week before returning to London, he went to see the nuns at the convent where he had spent his earliest schooldays under their tutelage. He would always remember it as a time of happiness. There had been a feeling of calm and security. Unlike some children, he looked forward to going to school. Every afternoon he skipped home already full of excited anticipation of the day to follow. Holidays were something he positively disliked, a time of enforced inactivity when he was never given the freedom to do what he liked. His home life as a child was uncompromisingly sterile, whereas at school he could participate in games, lessons and church services. He loved to pray surrounded by nuns, with a smell of incense pervading the church interior. His little body would shiver with infant sensuality so exquisite that it remained for ever in his memory.

The black habits of the nuns, those beautiful creatures who had renounced earthly pleasures and comfort to dedicate their bodies and souls to God, seemed to screen him from the world outside. There was a warmth and piety that held for the child a quality of fairytale innocence which by its very nature he could never experience in his life again. As he returned to the convent after so long an absence, he was amazed to be instantly recognized by the sisters, who greeted him with rapturous joy. Words failed him for once; he was too overcome to express how deeply this reception moved him. For days afterwards memories of the visit, and the nuns' unaffected happiness at seeing him again, sent echoes of pleasure racing through his mind.

By now Lara and her sister were back in Cambridge and his own departure was imminent. The boy's father booked his return itinerary through the same travel agent who had arranged the previous journey. The parting from his family was an emotional one, and he turned to mount the gangplank amid a profusion of goodbyes and tears. This time he was going on board a luxurious modern Italian ship. It was on its way to Venice.

This voyage was to be a much more relaxing affair than any of his previous sea-going experiences. The boy felt calm in himself, and more confident. He was looking forward to being back in London and had none of the worries that had overshadowed his first trip. Now he knew exactly where he was heading and the reception that awaited him. That he had made many friends in London meant that his life in the great city was destined to become more exciting by the day. He made up his mind he would rest for the five days at sea, so as to feel reinvigorated by the time he reached his destination.

On board the brand-new ship everything was gleaming. The boy was content just to sit in a deckchair in the sun, reading a book or chatting with his fellow passengers. The ship engendered such a friendly atmosphere that everyone sailing in her seemed to be enjoying themselves. Crossing the Mediterranean at this leisurely pace in perfect summer conditions relaxed the mind and refreshed the spirit in a most therapeutic way. Mealtimes were important occasions. The passengers counted the hours in anticipation, and when the dining-room doors were opened, there was always an unseemly dash to get served first. The diners devoured their food like a starving mob suddenly faced with a mountain of plenty. The meals were certainly delicious, with incomparable pasta hors-d'oeuvres sharpening the appetite for the delights to come.

Three days into the trip, and there had been no incidents to ruffle the calm surface. The beautiful weather continued, and after sundown the night sky became a canopy of stars. The boy would sit on deck in the dark for a long time each evening, reluctant to go down to his cabin and shut the door. On the fourth night, as he was watching the evening sea and sky at their most glorious, he became aware of a couple close by who were having a furious argument. It ended with the man walking away in a state of high agitation, while the woman remained standing where she was, clutching the ship's rail. The boy could see she was crying. After several minutes, he stood up and moved closer; then he asked if she needed help. She mumbled something slightly incoherent in reply, but the boy understood that he was not intruding, and that if he wanted to keep her company, she would not be averse to it.

After they had spoken for a little while, the woman began to recover herself. She explained that she was a doctor from Argentina who had been attending an international seminar in Israel. Her plan had been to take a short break in Europe in company with a man she had met at the seminar; the same one with whom she had just been quarrelling. Now the relationship was over and she would have to go alone. The boy commiserated with her over her spoilt plans, but she retorted briskly that people had to take such reversals in their stride and improvise as the need arose. By close to midnight they had talked for almost two hours. As they bade each other good night, they promised to meet again next morning. The boy had told her all she needed to know about himself; there they left matters for the time being.

The next day when they met again as arranged, she threw him into utter confusion by asking him to accompany her on the planned tour of Europe. The trip would be a short one, she explained – no longer than ten days. She was expected back in her home country shortly. The boy was staggered by the offer. His first thought was that he had very little spare money and could not afford to go anywhere except straight to London as planned, but she overcame these misgivings by saying that if he accepted the invitation she would pay for the entire trip.

His mind went back to Lara, from whom he had parted so recently. Somewhat older than Lara, the Argentinian doctor was in her early thirties. She had a shapely figure and a pretty face. Lara had the strong features often associated with firmness of character and single-mindedness. She also had the semitic glow that young Jewish women possess in their teens and that remains with them till full maturity. Lara's radiance was in fact exceptional, but, because she was older, the doctor possessed a greater sophistication and the air of a woman endowed with worldly wisdom.

While he had felt extremely fond of Lara, he knew in his heart of hearts that their relationship could only be short-lived because their lives were so different. The age gap between them as a couple had been slight, but the cultural divide was wide. There was little hope that bridging this would be easy. However, the doctor from Argentina, the boy reflected, was really quite attractive as an older woman. It would have been churlish, even crazy, to refuse the invitation. Experience with an older woman, especially a doctor, could not fail to advance his education *vis-à-vis* the opposite sex. As he accepted the offer of being a travelling companion, without reflecting on the possible consequences, an expression of relief came over the doctor's face and she kissed him in her excitement.

When the ship docked at Venice, the doctor insisted they take a gondola to their hotel. It was the most con-venient way to travel in the city, besides being the most elegant. As the gondola made its way through the narrow, winding canals, the boy gazed in wonder at the grandeur and picturesque decadence he saw all around him; he was intrigued and enchanted by the mysterious old houses leaning over waterways that served the function of streets. The hotel was a haunt of the rich and famous, renowned for its decor and impeccable service. They were allocated a magnificent double room with a view over the water that was breathtaking. He was at once alive to the majesty of Venice and could not stop exclaiming at its beauty and ancient architecture. He was also aware that he would be expected to earn his keep, one way or another, in the large double bed. He felt some apprehension over what was in store for him, but while the prospect, he calculated, could have its downside, it should also have its rewards.

As soon as they had settled in, they set off on the first of several tours of discovery. They went all over the city on foot, or sometimes took a gondola to negotiate particular areas that were more accessible by water. They visited all the famous sights, such as St Mark's Basilica, and went shopping for Venetian handicrafts, especially leather goods, which the doctor loved. At frequent intervals she insisted on buying the boy a gift, to remind him, so she said, of the wonderful days they were spending together in the city of the doges. Before they went out to dinner, on that and every evening, she gave him a wad of notes to ensure he had enough money to take care of the bill.

Her sense of what was correct in her comportment in public places could not be faulted. She dressed well, in conventional fashion, with nothing overpowering or showy. The expensive quality of her clothes ensured that her general appearance was smart yet low key. It was in the bedroom, as the boy had expected, that she gave rein to the flamboyant side of her nature. The doctor's collection of seductive cotton and silk lingerie was fabulous. There was no failure of taste, but provocation was undoubtedly high on the agenda.

[47]

A routine for their afternoons soon developed. After a good lunch, with several glasses of fine Italian wine, which the doctor always chose with care from the menu, she insisted they should have a siesta for an hour. Once this was over, she would take a bubble bath for twenty minutes, returning to bed with a towel wrapped round her waist, which she then flipped away to reveal her naked body. The immediate impression was of the glistening freshness possessed by a certain type of woman. Her skin looked soft and alluring; her breasts, small and firm, were enhanced by pinkish nipples that seemed permanently erect.

To begin the proceedings, the doctor would ask the boy to rub her whole body with a kind of aromatic oil that she always had with her. She orchestrated every move. First he must rub one of her breasts, then the other, gently, with the most delicate touch, applying no pressure whatsoever. The softer the touch, the more appreciative she grew. Then she instructed him how to massage her inner thighs in the vicinity of her vagina, using a teasing irregularity. She spread her legs to give his hands easier access. At times she would tell him to stop, but only to pause before he moved on to another area. All of this was part of the prelude before the real action began. The process was a lengthy one, involving no haste. It had to be executed in such a way as to prolong her sense of gratification.

She appeared to be well versed in the arts of love. After every short interlude she urged him to wet his lips with saliva and rub them tenderly against her nipples while, with her own hand, she caressed her clitoris. Visibly excited by now, she asked the boy to remove his clothes and lie next to her. As he lay there naked, she ran her tongue all over his body, giving little bites from time to time and making his genitals convulse with fluttering touches from her fingers. The boy, in a heightened state of arousal, wondered how he could contain himself. As he sought to possess her, she wriggled her body and crossed her legs teasingly to prevent it. She continued for some time, alternately curbing his arousal then reinflaming it, till every nerve in his body was trembling with desire. As soon as she sensed he had reached this point, she allowed him freedom of movement. His thrust into her body was deep and intense. As they reached mutual orgasm it seemed that their intimate fluids mingled. For ten minutes afterwards both felt utterly exhausted and drained and could hardly move.

This process, always leading to a frenzied climax, was repeated on three consecutive afternoons. At night, things took on a more down-to-earth dimension. Returning to the room after dinner, having consumed a fair amount of wine, they would collapse on the bed, refrain from all foreplay, and simply fuck till sleep overcame them. The boy was at an age when he was at his sexual peak, but he was beginning to find it impossible to keep up with the doctor's insatiable demands for more; less would have made life easier where he was concerned. His energies were beginning to desert him. He wondered how much longer he could cope with this situation. The punishing schedule was beginning to take its toll, and they started to bicker as small resentments began to surface. Still, there was the positive side. She was teaching him how to delay his orgasm; how to climax simultaneously with a sexual partner. It was a matter of mind over body, she told him. You can control it by switching your mind completely away, turning your thoughts to other subjects and blotting out your surroundings.

Tantric sex, the doctor claimed, could be achieved by applying yoga to the mind as well as to the body. You had to persevere to master it. She was confident that she could teach the boy how to perfect it. The challenge for him to control his ejaculation was painfully difficult at first, and his natural impatience did not help matters. Then, with each lesson, his anxiety about his orgasmic function began to simmer down.

He began to understand how, with women and sex, it was futile to hurry matters. The process had to be allowed to take its natural course. A languid approach was more desirable than an urgent one. It was important to create the right atmosphere of eroticism. Women, he soon realized, have a different perspective from men on many things, their physical needs in general being tempered by their emotional ones. It was necessary for sex to be savoured like a good meal if its life force was to be appreciated. Yet the doctor had become remorseless in driving things forward towards the ultimate goal of a complementary physical union.

Despite his growing worries about being able to maintain the pace she was setting in bed, the boy continued to enjoy the doctor's company. As the shopping sprees went on each day, he delighted in her conversation. They discovered they had much in common, sharing an interest in art, books and cultural activities, not to mention good food and wine. She also showed a sympathy for the

Palestinians' struggle for statehood, having seen their plight at first hand during her brief stay in Israel. Besides all this, there was the constantly unfolding panorama of Venice with its fascinating history. It had started to come into being soon after ad 450, when fugitives from the invasions by the Germanic Lombard tribes from the north took refuge among an archipelago of about a hundred small islands in a lagoon on the Adriatic coast. Gradually the settlements achieved cohesion and identity with a system of bridges and canals and the population mushroomed. By the Middle Ages, Venice was established as a proudly independent city-state, governed by its doge (the equivalent of a duke) and vastly influential as a maritime power.

Life in Venice revolved around the glorious Piazza San Marco, the symbol of the city for over a thousand years. The piazza was the beating heart of the city's public life. It was a revelation for the boy to see it in all its phases, but especially when it was at its most colourful in the early morning light; or at dusk, when the mosaics of St Mark's Basilica came to life and the adjoining buildings began to glow with a golden warmth. The boy and the doctor spent many hours in the piazza, marvelling at its Byzantine splendour. As a romantic experience it was incomparable with anything else the boy had known. Venice entranced his vision and his senses. It had everything imaginable to offer. Through its historic link with the Ottomans, it fused Eastern craftsmanship with Western elegance. It was as if the two worlds intertwined to produce the best of each in a kaleidoscope of colour and design. No wonder those who had lived there and loved it had called it La

Serenissima. The whole city struck him as being like a vast, beautiful vessel afloat in the often calm waters of the Adriatic. It was a rich treasure, every facet of which, to his innocent eye, combined in a vibrancy of effect that he knew he would never be able to recapture.

From Venice the boy and the doctor travelled on to Florence. Here things improved in their relationship. Their love-making took on a more relaxed tempo. The urgency of the doctor's ardour seemed to diminish; her drive for sexual excess to grow less insistent. For the boy it made a welcome change and he breathed a sigh of relief to himself, thinking the height of her fervour might be passed. They stopped snapping at each other under the stress of her unreasonable physical demands. The situation grew calmer, and strangely enough it began to feel more fulfilling. They started to go about Florence with increased zest and savoured every moment of being together. Love in the afternoon was dispensed with. They had too many other distractions as they tried to get round all the art galleries and shops for which the city was renowned. Everywhere they went there were artisan craftsmen working in their individual workshops, producing items of jewellery in gold or silver, or leatherwear, or decorative glassware.

There was one teacher the boy had been very keen on when he was at school who would often talk to him about Naples and Florence and their place in history. It had been a dream that he might visit both cities one day, and now the dream was being fulfilled in the case of Florence. What was more, the visit was being made in style, since the doctor had the means to demand the best. He could not believe his good fortune. Here he was in the city where, during the Renaissance, the ruling family of merchant bankers, the Medici, had used their wealth and patronage to make it a centre of art and learning. The Florentines in their day had been pre-eminent in appreciating the importance for humanity of the driving forces of imagination and intellect. The poet Dante was a native of the city, though forced to live some of his life away from it for political reasons. Brunelleschi had invented modern perspective there and designed the great dome of the cathedral. Giotto established a new realism in fresco painting in the church of Santa Croce. Leonardo and Michelangelo came to the city to work. Galileo defined many of the principles of modern science in Florence, under the protecting auspices of the Medici – though ultimately they could not save him from the persecution of the Inquisition and he was forced to recant his confirmation of Copernicus's theory that the earth moves round the sun.

A catalogue of facts about Florence went spinning through the boy's head. He had no way of guessing what an important focus for many of his activities the city would become some thirty years later when he ran a conglomerate dealing with luxury goods and fine textiles. In those days to come he would be visiting Florence on a regular basis, seeking to buy and market the finest of hand-crafted artefacts that their manufacturers could offer. Similarly he could not know, as he stood and admired a handsome Tuscan villa called La Pietra, which looked out over the city from its imposing hillside position, that this too would play a part in his future life. It stood behind its imposing iron gates, beyond a grand approach of stone steps and balustrades, surrounded by a marvellous garden, landscaped with trees, shrubs and statuary. La Pietra was the home of the Actons, whose familial links with Florence and the rest of Italy went back for well over a century. It housed one of the finest private collections of art and antiques ever assembled.

The assembling had been done by Arthur Acton, a businessman and speculator, and his American wife Hortense. The old couple still lived in their fifty-four-room palace at the time with their son Harold. In his wildest dreams the boy never imagined that a day would come when he would be invited there as a guest of Sir Harold Acton, as he later became, and forge with him a friendship that would last for the rest of Sir Harold's life. Harold was one of the outstanding scholars and raconteurs of his generation, though he did not come into the freedom of his full inheritance until after the death of his mother at the age of ninety. Right to the end she never trusted him with his own latchkey – but such odd stories awaited discovery a good way along the road ahead.

In the evenings on this first visit to Florence, the boy and the doctor dined in style at fashionable restaurants and sipped vintage Italian wines till late in the evening. The boy, who was not accustomed to heavy drinking, was always tipsy as they negotiated their way back to their hotel. Generally, once in the room, they would hurriedly dispose of their clothes and just collapse on the bed, lying flat out as the night ticked by. Yet, however profoundly asleep he was, he would be remorselessly roused to semi-consciousness in the small hours as her roving hands explored his body and its sexual state. Then, somehow or other, he would find himself manoeuvring to perch on top of her and thump away, unable to tell whether he was groaning in ecstasy or pain.

Paris was the next and final stop on their European tour; from there he would be heading home to London. As they travelled together, they seemed to all outward appearances a contented couple despite the age gap. They demonstrably shared a mutual affection. Differences there may have been in private, especially in the confines of the bedroom, but in their quieter moments they were aware they had achieved an intimacy of rare quality.

Paris brought with it a new range of experience. The boy at once felt at home there because he could speak the language fluently. The great metropolis, with its magnificent avenues and boulevards, famous river embankments and cosmopolitan atmosphere, was a city universally celebrated and admired. To be able to stroll along the Champs-Élysées was the fulfilment of a dream for the boy. The traffic, the cafés, the multitudes of people promenading, made the air vibrate with excitement. Impressive monuments, depicting the glories of the history and culture of a great nation, were to be seen everywhere. They travelled by foot, by Métro, by taxi. They went everywhere in a sort of frenzy, racing against the clock to absorb everything they could in the little time they had left. At the outset, sightseeing became their priority and sex was put on hold. Even the delicious French cuisine, to be discovered at its best in so many back-street bistros, was accorded scant attention.

For two days their relationship was relaxed and harmonious. Then, without warning, the doctor's carnal demons returned with redoubled force. Love in the afternoon was back and making imperious demands. Her attitude changed and her focus became predatory. The boy sensed he was being called on to service something that was more an addiction than a need. He was naturally attracted towards sexual activity, but by now he had experienced a surfeit of it with the doctor. The relationship was starting to have a disturbing effect on his psyche. The bedroom rows that followed began to brew up into an unpleasant atmosphere. His instincts told him that, however skilled the seduction, these emotional coercions to make love when he was exhausted, or in an inappropriate state of mind, could leave him with a legacy of damage. The adventure had to be terminated; it was a matter of self-preservation.

One day he went back to the hotel alone and packed his only suitcase. He did not wait for her so they could say goodbye; a parting in those circumstances was not something he could handle. He left for the boat-train, but all the way, as the journey put distance between them, the doctor from Latin America and the unexpected way they had become lovers dominated his thoughts. He recalled her generosity with affection, and was grateful for the way she had looked after him during the ten days they had spent together. But in the end, he had had no alternative except to run away. He was being drained physically and mentally and had grown fearful of where it all might lead.

Despite the intimacy the boy had known with the Argentinian doctor, she remained a rather mysterious figure in his mind. He had learnt nothing about her family background, except that it was quite obvious that she had been born into a moneyed, cultured household. She rarely talked about herself and was evasive if the boy ever tried to probe for information. It was as if she had somehow wanted to remain anonymous. She never even discussed her work as a doctor, except that she mentioned tending the poor free of charge once a week to make a contribution to society. Every item about her person reflected wealth, style and good taste, yet she refused to flaunt it or draw attention to it in any way. She was very diffident in herself, but her personality was striking. Her elegant bearing and animated features made her a centre of attention, though it was nothing she sought or wished for. It simply happened that her physical presence defined her in any setting and she seemed to draw everything to her without making the slightest effort. She remained composed, disciplined and self-assured in every public situation.

Her politics were a topic that she did freely discuss with the boy. She showed a sympathetic understanding of the plight of the underprivileged and cited the Palestinians as a prime example among those who had lost out in the international game of *realpolitik*. She was certainly with the underdog and it was clear on which side of the barricades she would fight if it ever came to revolution. Nevertheless she was completely unself-conscious about enjoying the comforts of her status and wealth. The contradiction, if it even existed, was somehow not an issue in her case. When her excessive physical demands were in abeyance, it was a delight to be in her company. The boy learned so much from her in such a brief period of time. It was tutoring of a rare and special kind that few young men have the good fortune to encounter in their formative years. The boy knew it. During those few days his life was enriched in ways that ranged from the ridiculous to the sublime, and stoically he accepted that both extremes were necessary. He could not have one without the other. In a unique way they became strangely complementary.

He had grown up in an essentially puritan society. Sex was never discussed in his family or his social milieu. It was certainly not looked on as a joyful function, worthy of exploration, and it remained the forbidden fruit. The Roman Catholic Church accepted it only grudgingly as the means of creating new life, since no other method of procreation was possible. The one exception had been in the case of the Virgin Mary, the mother of Christ, who was impregnated by the Holy Spirit without any intervention on the part of her husband Joseph. The mere fact that, among all the saints, the Virgin Mary was the most revered, just went to illustrate how the tenets of the New Testament were anti-sex in their underlying emphasis. What logic was there in a view that abstention and suffering rather than joy and well-being lay at the core of salvation? Throughout his adolescence he had struggled to understand how it was that sex must be condemned to be hedged about with guilt and frowned upon as a necessary evil when it was the lifeblood of existence, something to be celebrated rather than rejected. He could never arrive at a convincing answer. Without sex, the world would come to an end; without sex to fuel it, the drive to achieve ever greater objectives and ambitions must run down and fizzle out. The joys of nurturing a life conceived in the fulfilling act of love would be unknown and humanity robbed of the essence of its reason for being.

The boy's upbringing had failed to brainwash him into denying the value of his sexuality. It always seemed to him that sex was beyond question the supreme mechanism for maintaining a healthy body and giving it energy and direction. In his childhood, he had desperately sought to plumb the depths of the religious mysteries, but he always came back to the truth of the fact that if he accidentally caught a glimpse of the sparkling white flesh of a woman's inner thighs his male organ would start to rise and expand; or if he touched himself in a state of arousal, the liquid that stained his trousers represented the relief that came so strangely and was not to be denied. In this way, he acquired an inkling of the joys sex had to offer before he knew what they really meant or could exploit them to the full.

His initiation into the higher subtleties of sex at the hands of the Argentinian doctor came not only as a revelation but also as a unique experience that would mould his sexuality for all the years that lay ahead. She taught him everything she could about the female form, its secret urges and the way it functioned. She showed him how to respond to its needs and how not to be selfish or self-engrossed in seeking the ends of desire. Admittedly, she made him suffer. At times he was not up to the task, despite being, at his age, at the height of his sexual powers. Her needs, at that stage of her evolution in life, were greater than his. It was often a struggle for him to match her energy and keep her satisfied. His body would reach a point where it could no longer take the strain and he felt physical pain from excessive gratification. But the negative aspects of this epic sexual adventure, pursued through three great European cities, were more than counter-balanced by the deep knowledge with which she imbued him. He never denied that he remained grateful to her, for she had shaped him into the man he was to become: a man who liked and trusted women and was never to feel uncomfortable in their company.

The boy came back to the house in Munster Road that his uncle had found for them to share. It was a small terrace house, on two floors, and it had a back garden. The neighbours were friendly in the chirpy London way. They would always exchange a few words, mostly about the weather – the perennial British obsession – before going on their cheerful way. The new polytechnic term had just begun, and the boy cycled to college each morning, leaving the house at about 8.30. The journey took him half an hour or so. He was normally home in the evenings by just before six. He enjoyed the exercise. It kept him slim and fit. He was by now heavily involved in his role as a table-tennis coach, besides playing for the polytechnic in competitive tournaments. His skills improved dramatically with the constant practice. The talent and tenacity he devoted to the game developed his style into one that was fast and furious, backed by a remarkable agility. He was successful in winning the table-tennis championship of the

University of London two years running, and was urged by some to turn professional. This he did for a while, but his enthusiasm soon flagged and he gave it up six months later for lack of commitment.

In the lecture rooms he was becoming less attentive. Little in the subject matter engaged his interest. He felt he was there under false pretences as he had never had any intention of becoming an engineer. Mechanical things held no attraction for him; more than that, he loathed the very thought of them. Back home his ambition had always been to become a journalist, but his father had other views on the subject. He knew of his son's sense of vocation for journalism, and had ample proof of the boy's ability and determination from an early age, but in the context of the Middle East it was a profession that could carry with it particular dangers. The political situation had been, and continued to be, precarious and characterized by blood-shed and spasmodic episodes of violence. Journalism was considered to be a hazardous occupation in a world where personal scores were often settled by the gun.

It was therefore inconceivable that his father, obsessively protective as he was, would ever consider journalism as a suitable occupation for his son, who was the only male in the family. It would have been tantamount to courting the boy's early death. The only way the boy was able to persuade his father to send him to England to complete his education had been on the pretext of wanting to become an engineer. The one qualification he possessed to justify this change of direction was his propensity for mathematics. At school, where he always came top of the class in maths, his class mates had referred to him as 'the wizard', and the accolade spilled over into his college days.

It was his strength in mathematics, in fact, that kept him afloat in the engineering course at the polytechnic, despite his substandard work in physics and chemistry. For these two subjects he felt no affinity whatsoever. To make matters worse, he could not suppress his boredom and impatience when conducting scientific experiments in the laboratory. He would abandon an experiment halfway through, making some excuse or other. His social life, by contrast, developed into a hectic round of activity. He channelled his ingenuities into finding ways to avoid work, flirting and devising time for recreational pursuits. As his life moved into the fast lane, he began to relish every minute of it.

His intimate circle of friends came to mean a great deal to him. His friends in turn introduced him to their parents. One such was Peter Garnett, who had been with him in the polytechnic preparatory school before graduating to the main college. Peter, who lived with his family in Maida Vale, had two younger brothers and a sister called Julie. Julie, the boy decided, in the terminology used by the young men of that generation, was quite a dish. She was to feature in the boy's life with some prominence for many years. Their father was known as 'Papp' Garnett.

Papp was an elderly gentleman with a sharp sense of humour. He had worked in the colonial service before the war and had been sent to Palestine during the British Mandate. As an engineer, he had been responsible for laying the first telephone system in Palestine and had been put in charge of postal communications. To lay the lines he had used convict labour. The convicts were able to earn substantial reductions in their sentences by undertaking the work; those guilty of minor crimes could be released on completing their contracts.

In an earlier marriage, in England, Papp had fathered four daughters and a son. His wife had died giving birth to the youngest child, a girl called Nadia, who was put out for adoption to a childless couple. The youngest of the three remaining girls, Grace, was her father's special favourite. The pattern of their life was for the children to join their father in Palestine just for the school holidays, but Grace was then allowed to stay on with him and go to school in the Holy Land when the others returned to England. At her school Grace made friends with a girl called Afifi whose eldest sister happened to be her father's house-keeper. At the age of twenty, Afifi became her father's new wife. Papp Garnett was at least twenty years her senior.

In the meantime, Grace fell in love with a Palestinian Arab boy and wanted to marry him. At this point, Papp's typically colonial double standards came into play and he objected strongly, seeking to thwart the union in every way possible. Grace was devastated at not being able to marry the man she truly loved. On the rebound, she accepted in desperation the proposal of a colleague of her father's, a man very much older than herself. Locked into a marriage with a husband she didn't love, she too died in childbirth. Papp mourned her death till the very end of his life.

Afifi, the mother of his second family, was Lebanese. She was totally devoted to Papp, whose response was to tease her mercilessly. But it was all done in good humour and the atmosphere in the house was never dull. There was always something going on and the house seemed to be constantly crowded with guests, who were all well looked after. Afifi spent most of her time in the kitchen, either preparing or serving food.

The boy became a regular visitor. Peter, who was the eldest son, often took him home straight from the polytechnic to have supper with the family. It was an open house, friendly and harmonious. The boy spent the night there on many occasions. Johnny, the middle brother, had a keen sense of mischief. He and the boy would go in search of William, the youngest brother of the three, to play tricks on him. William was then fourteen. If they found William asleep, they would push marbles into his mouth and watch as he struggled to rid himself of these foreign objects so rudely intruding into his slumbers. Suddenly William would rouse himself, still in a stupor, and lash out, shouting a string of obscenities that always ended with, 'Leave me alone, you bastards!'

Peter did not always approve of this treatment of his youngest brother and occasionally stirred up trouble for the tormentors by reporting them to Afifi. For Afifi, her youngest son was 'her darling William', for whom she had a specially soft spot, always calling him a 'good boy' no matter what he got up to. Afifi was a simple woman, good natured and hard working. In her young days in Lebanon girls left school rather early and did not have access to the benefits of higher education. She had a natural grasp of things and through intuition managed to overcome any of the disadvantages that might have held her back in the circumstances. To her children she was a wonderful mother in the old traditional way. She attended to their every need; she was a willing participant in their daily life, sharing in the fun and being teased into the bargain. She had a relaxed manner and was a generous soul who wished no harm to anyone.

Unlike many people who came from a similar background, Afifi possessed a great sense of humour. She was never inclined to dramatize things in a negative context, and could be relied on not to take umbrage over something that was only a silly incident or harmless prank. These she usually took in her stride, but when it came to William she was very protective. She made it clear to everyone that, where William was concerned, he should be left to his own devices and not be harassed. William was talented musically. He spent hours practising his saxophone, and was hounded by his brothers for the noise it made. Eventually he graduated to playing gigs in jazz clubs, subsidizing his income by repairing musical instruments.

The Garnett daughter, Julie, was sixteen, and like her deceased predecessor, Grace, was the apple of her father's eye. He had a way of doting on her and had cast her in the role of queen bee, a part she was happy to play. As the boy virtually became one of the Garnett family, his relationship with Julie was on an equal level with the one he had with her brothers. Yet, as they did more things together, she became his real focus of attention. The boy loved her as he would a sister. They grew to be very close, exchanged secrets and told each other jokes. If they were apart, as when the boy was away, they corresponded on a regular basis. They were never romantically linked; it was an enduring relationship that was precious in its own right.

Life in Munster Road was uneventful compared with the scene at the Garnetts' in Maida Vale. The boy's uncle conversed little. He also had to swat hard for his exams, being a slow learner, and he needed to put more effort into his studies than his fellow students. He worked slowly and methodically. His vocabulary recognized no short cuts, and to a casual observer it would have seemed that in his thought processes he always took the longest possible route to arrive at a conclusion. He had no specific hobbies to amuse himself with, and any spare time was spent languidly fiddling with household fixtures that he thought needed attention. As a companion, he was predictably reliable, but in terms of entertainment value he was hopeless. The boy had to admit that his uncle generally tried to please, though there was always something irritating in the way he went about it. A certain impervious charm showed itself only intermittently.

The boy hardly ever stayed in for the evenings at Munster Road, but preferred to mix with his inner circle of friends from college. He cut through his homework rapidly; it took him no time to zero in on the essence of its subject matter and get to the nub of the whole exercise in question. It was impossible for the boy and his uncle to ignore their differences. Instead, for the sake of cordial relations, they agreed to disagree on most issues. In this both showed a healthy, mature regard for opposing views, which only went to prove that conflict is avoidable where common sense prevails against discord.

There was only one distraction in the boy's emotional life at this time, and she took the form of a Belgian girl he met on one of his outings. She was in London to study

English and was close to the end of a six-month course. Her family was reasonably well off and she possessed all the right credentials for getting on in society. There were no pretensions attached to the signs of breeding she displayed: immaculate manners and a dress sense in keeping with the times, yet always understated and smart. Her sweet nature exuded innocence, which enhanced her sex appeal in a way that was quite unintentional.

The boy admired her for her pretty face, her shapely contours and her lyrically soft voice, that came across as perhaps her most alluring feature. Yet his wild exploits with the Argentinian doctor remained indelibly stamped on his mind. He had a sense that any sexual engagement in this case was likely to seem at best a polite exercise in good manners. The girl was to prove his instincts right: her refined, gentle approach to intimacy lacked any aggressive demands. She was able to offer moments of intense sensuality and unalloyed pleasure, but the relationship did not last. She returned to Belgium after a few days, and sent him a postcard, but after that there was silence, followed by another silence. The chapter was closed.

With a long holiday break from the polytechnic coming up, the boy took a job with a company called Phillips Mills. It was located on the River Thames, next to Battersea Bridge, and its work was to collect wastepaper and string for recycling. Part of the boy's duties was to assist the van driver in collecting and loading big bags of wastepaper and string from various shops and offices throughout the London area. In the course of the day, they also collected a quantity of tips, which they divided equally. If they were given a small packet of Woodbines containing five cigarettes, they would cut one cigarette in half to make the equation balance.

The boy enjoyed being a driver's mate. The work was physical and sometimes tiring, but the changes of scenery made it enjoyable. The less congenial part of his duties was the many days he had to spend in the sorting office, endlessly untying knotted string. He thought it would send him mad. Indeed, he noticed how the few people who worked there on a permanent basis, untying knots all day, were in the habit of talking to themselves. Either it was their way of letting off steam, or, more probably, they had been damaged mentally by the stultifying boredom of the job. After only about ten days of this particular work, the boy found that he too was becoming deranged and had started talking to himself. Clearly the time had come for him to leave.

He still saw Miss Willmott on a regular basis, and their close relationship had lost none of its warmth. She was well settled in Streatham and had no regrets about leaving the house in Oakley Gardens. In fact she had always found that Chelsea, with its gatherings of artists and writers and its bohemian atmosphere, was somewhat incompatible with her more conservative view of life. With her wish to return to Streatham fulfilled, she now had no need to take in lodgers to pay for the upkeep of her house, and was happy and contented as a result. She was able to devote more time to the care of the blind man and his wife. Having reached a certain age, they now needed more looking after than ever. Her job with Miss Newton was also less stressful. She had been able to reduce it to two days a week on account of the distance.

The boy had remained one of Miss Newton's habitual visitors too. Miss Newton remained as sharp-minded and eccentric as she had ever been. She continued to indulge him out of her bag of tricks, from bottles of whisky to cakes, or with advances for items of clothing that she decided he needed, depending on her mood of the day. Her generosity and benevolence were something he accepted with his customary easy grace. Any refusal would have infuriated her. She was a woman accustomed to getting her own way in most things, and placing obstacles in her chosen path would never have gone down well.

On one of his visits to Miss Newton's, the boy met a journalist called George Hutchinson, who worked on the 'Londoner's Diary' column of the *Evening Standard*. George impressed him as a dashing young man with impeccable breeding. He struck the boy at once as the type of Englishman about whom you read in books – one with immaculate manners and *savoir faire*. He moved about the room, with a cigarette in one hand and a glass of whisky in the other, preserving perfect poise and resembling one of the heroes in a Noël Coward play. Despite this aristocratic air, he came from a humble Yorkshire background, as the boy would discover in due course. He spoke softly and listened attentively to what anyone else was saying; he was never abrasive or melodramatic in his observations. In fact he had a refreshing coolness that disarmingly concealed an intrinsic warmth of character. There was not a fibre of malice or deviousness in George's being. He was as straight in his dealings with others as anyone could possibly be.

Miss Newton was very fond of George. It was clear they took immense pleasure in each other's company. There was an affinity that bridged the age divide in all their discussions. George was a fine writer. He was economical with words, which he used concisely to convey precise meaning. His style was compact and non-repetitious. He would often agonize over finding the right form for a phrase or sentence, for he constantly strove to honour the English language by adhering to its correct usage. In some ways, he was an old-fashioned traditionalist, though he often wrote with a progressive insight that was ahead of its time. His political judgement was sharp and rarely in error. As a columnist, he won a loyal readership across the generations, and his appeal was nationwide.

When the boy first met George, his career as a journalist was very much in the ascendant. He had been working on a ship as a merchant seaman when the great press baron of the day, Lord Beaverbrook, happened to come on board and noticed him. George thus became one of Beaver-brook's protégés and was obviously destined for great things. He was to assume an important role in the boy's early days in England, and in the years to follow their professional lives would intertwine in various unexpected ways.

Meanwhile, back in Munster Road, the boy's uncle was growing restless. He resented having to pay rent, which he considered an unnecessary waste of money, and had set his heart on buying a property. Houses at the time were really quite cheap, but, on the other hand, very little cash was available for raising capital. The property market was basically a seller's market, and the uncle had no money of his own. He therefore suggested to the boy that he talk to Papp Garnett, who seemed to be comfortably off, though no one had any idea whether this was indeed the case. The boy therefore approached Papp Garnett and found him receptive to the idea. Papp's condition for agreeing to lend the money was that any property must be worth what was paid for it. The boy's uncle therefore set off on another house-hunting search, which ended when he came across a house in Geraldine Road, just off East Hill, Wandsworth. Though it was not freehold, it had a long lease. It took his fancy and was within his budget of £1,000; undoubtedly, it was a bargain.

The reason for the house being such good value was that the basement and the ground floor were occupied by protected tenants who paid a nominal rent. In the basement lived a fireman and his young family, while a single elderly lady occupied the ground floor. This left available for accommodation the rest of the house, which consisted of a small mezzanine used as a kitchen and a first and second floor with two rooms each. The main drawback was that there was, for all the occupants, just one bathroom, and this incorporated the only lavatory. In those days it was not unusual for one bathroom and a single lavatory to be shared by a number of tenants in a rented property, but this would be an unacceptable arrangement by modern standards of hygiene. Nothing daunted, the boy's uncle completed the purchase with the help of Papp Garnett, and he and the boy moved from Parsons Green to Geraldine Road.

The change of address involved a need for further adjustments. For one thing, there was a new arrival in the household. The uncle invited a former colleague, a fellow student he had met at college in Bournemouth some years before, to come and lodge with them. The understanding was that the new lodger and the boy would pay a weekly sum to cover rent, food, fuel and electricity and enable the uncle to reduce his debt to Papp Garnett on a regular basis. At this particular time, the boy had no problems with money. Ever since he arrived in England, he had been receiving a monthly allowance of £30 from his father. It was more than adequate. He could live on it quite comfortably and even have money to spare for an occasional binge. In addition to this allowance, there was the cash that Miss Newton stuffed surreptitiously into his pockets at the end of every one of his visits. Once he discovered that she had pressed on him a present of £50. When he counted the notes he was flabbergasted. This was a great deal of money at a time when you could purchase a house like the one in Geraldine Road for £1,000.

The biggest adjustment of all involved the primitive bathroom arrangements. If the lavatory was in use, access to the bathroom was blocked; if someone was having a bath, entry to the lavatory was equally out of the question. Putting up with these cumbersome and sometimes embarrassing inconveniences required at times a super-human level of commitment to cooperative living.

The new lodger was called Stinous. He was a Greek Cypriot who suffered from stomach ulcers. He therefore had to be careful with his diet, and more often than not ate the wrong food and suffered the consequences, putting further strain on the bathroom arrangements. Unlike the boy's uncle, Stinous was full of fun. Although he was of the uncle's generation, and eleven years older than the boy, he became a willing participant in any pranks and devilry that the boy initiated. It was always debatable which of the two had the worse influence on the other. Their bonding in mischief caused several disruptions in the household.

Among the boy's friends at the polytechnic was a student whose father worked at a fireworks factory. With Guy Fawkes Night approaching, the friend came into college one day with a variety of high-quality fireworks. They were quite powerful, and were guaranteed to enthral any audience with a stunning display of colour and some satisfying explosions. The boy was happy to purchase a few items. The idea was starting to form in his mind that they could be a source of amusement and hilarity on the fifth of November. He calculated that if he placed them at the back of the fireplace he would have time to evacuate the living-room before the inevitable conflagration went off skywards. The fire was always laid ready to be lit each evening, for the uncle liked the sight of burning coal, especially during the long winter evenings.

Unbeknown to the boy, the uncle was expecting a monk and a priest to be making a social visit on that evening of 5 November. Only when the boy had put the fireworks in place, in accordance with his original plan, did the doorbell ring and the men of God arrive. There was no time for him to warn the uncle of impending disaster. The visitors were shown into the very room that was prepared for the spectacular surprise. Worse still, for some unknown reason, since it was not a particularly cold night, the priest rose and stood with his back to the fire to warm his behind as the merry flames took hold. The eruption in the fireplace, as the fireworks fizzed and banged up the chimney, singed his trousers and flung burning coals out on to the carpet.

Pandemonium ensued and the priest and the monk went simultaneously into a state of shock. They gibbered incoherently as the uncle, yellow with rage, distractedly ran back and forth, trying to contain the damage to the carpet by dousing it with a bucket of water. He was at a loss to fathom out what on earth was happening – the words 'terrorist attack' were not in those days part of the general vocabulary. The boy scurried off in utter panic, while Stinous, stunned by the turn the incident had taken, locked himself in his room to avoid the ugly confrontation that he knew must surely follow. Meanwhile the uncle tried to pacify and reassure his visitors with a litany of apologies, but all in vain. The priest and the monk left in complete disarray, humiliated and outraged. What was to have been a pleasant introductory visit to raise the tone of the ménage in spiritual matters had turned into the stuff of nightmare.

It was an affront to decency, the uncle raged once the whole picture became clear. It was a deliberate attack perpetrated against faithful servants of the church. In this he did the boy an injustice. No harm of the sort had been intended. The boy had known nothing of the impending visit, and had merely hoped to create a rumpus that would be an amusing diversion, a joke to savour. There was no denying that in this case it had badly misfired. The damage it caused to the relationship between the boy and his uncle and Stinous took a great deal of time and effort to repair.

Sexual activities were seldom a prominent feature of

life in Geraldine Road, but then, to everyone's surprise, the uncle brought home a cockney girl of twenty-seven called Rita. She was someone with a lot of spark and an easy-going nature. She was game for a laugh, and for anything else so long as it had an outrageous element to it. Although they seemed an unlikely couple, the uncle and Rita seemed to blend in a funny sort of way. The boy took to Rita. She was undoubtedly attractive. Her bosom was an asset of which she took good care, enhancing its appeal by the way she dressed. It projected quite tastefully but with tantalising effect. The rest of her was not short on womanly appeal either. In fact Rita was all woman, oozing the sort of sex appeal that men yearn after for its very rawness. The boy was unable to resist on more than one occasion asking her whether she had managed to sleep with his uncle, but the answer was always in the negative. The uncle remained very awkward and shy with women, while his religious conditioning dictated abstinence from any physical gratification.

Rita's style of elocution was East Endish, though it had an added resonance that defied classification. When she spoke, her voice was easy on the ear. The more the boy got to know her, the more he liked her; the more he liked her, the more he thought he would not mind bedding her if only it weren't for her relationship with the uncle. Inevitably the idea lingered in his imagination for a while. His intuition told him that the experience might be terrific. In his perception of Rita, he saw her as a woman for all seasons, one to be savoured and relished and not kept selfishly by one man for himself. Nevertheless, despite all the pressures to the contrary, he steadfastly refused to succumb to temptation. The seduction of Rita was ultimately confined to his dreams.

There was one occasion when the boy believed he saw Rita and his uncle kissing, but it was clear it went no further. On another occasion, after Rita had had a drop or two more to drink than usual, she confessed, without much probing, that the most they had done sexually was to cuddle half naked in bed. The uncle had apparently nestled his head on her naked breast; but, aroused and sweating profusely, he would go no further. Penetration outside the marital bed would be to him a mortal sin. He believed that the ultimate rewards of heaven must not be sacrificed for unsanctioned pleasurable encounters on earth. Stinous and the boy disagreed with this when they discussed the question between themselves. To them it seemed preferable to have it the other way round. It was far better, they maintained, to enjoy what could be felt and savoured in the here and now rather than look forward to hypothetical gratification in the future. As the saying went, a bird in the hand was worth two in the bush.

But Stinous, too, was an odd fish. The boy found him full of paradoxes. He was clever and studious at the same time as being worldly and a good companion to have around. He could be gregarious while remaining a solitary, self-sufficient character. He mixed well in a crowd, yet still looked lost. He could participate in the merriment of others without seeming to have any of his own. The boy tried to figure him out, but failed. Stinous rarely divulged anything about himself, though he was not shy and often expressed an opinion with considerable articulacy. He was rarely to be seen in the company of women and whether or not he had relationships with girls no one knew. The boy was unable to make any judgement on this score since he never saw him with a girlfriend. If he was sexually driven in any way, there were no outward signs. You could only say he was extremely nice but hard to decipher.

Stinous had many friends in Sheffield. The city had been his first stop in England when he came from Cyprus to study. His landlady of the time still took in lodgers, and one day she invited Stinous to come and visit for a long weekend with his two friends – meaning the uncle and the boy. It was a marvellous opportunity for the boy to see Sheffield and have a change of scene, which was something he needed at the time. He took at once to Stinous's former landlady, who was warm, jolly and direct, and had a wicked sense of humour. As a result, the boy, Stinous and the landlady ganged up on the uncle and started teasing him for his obvious piety and stuffy self-control, along with his awkwardness with the opposite sex.

As luck would have it, two of the current lodgers in the house were young women students who happened to be around for that weekend. They joined in the fun, and one of them struck the boy instantly as having the most enchanting good looks and poise. She had the sort of waif-like appearance which is devastatingly attractive in a completely natural, uncontrived way. The boy fell for her in a big way and the attraction seemed to be mutual, though to an outside observer it might have seemed that the boy was the more smitten of the two. From the moment he met the girl, he could not bear to be apart from her for a single hour.

Now it was his turn to have to endure much ribbing.

He took it all uncomplainingly. He was under her spell completely. The trams in Sheffield ran round the clock, so they took to the trams at night, visiting all the city nightspots and snatching every opportunity to cuddle in some dark corner or other. It was the sort of *coup de foudre* that by its very nature he knew couldn't last. So he must make the most of it. During the three days fate had allotted them, they made love whenever they could with such passion that it left him sizzling with the after-effects for days once he had returned to London. For a short while he and the girl corresponded, but the passion had departed as swiftly as it had seized them. Both became preoccupied with other more pressing matters and carried on with the business of living. The intensity of their meeting became a distant memory; it had been a long weekend of sheer ecstasy, dreamlike but divorced from reality.

Life in Geraldine Road settled back into its mundane routine. The kitchen was small and cosy at least. The three of them used to gather there for the evening meal. The uncle was chef and took great pride in his cooking. As in everything else he did, he was meticulous and slow. Most of the dishes he produced were judged a success, even if his repertoire was lacking in variety. Their staple diet consisted mainly of chicken and potatoes or sardines. Occasionally a roasted leg of lamb would be served at the weekend.

Conversations at the supper table were devoted mostly to life at the polytechnic, with special emphasis on how ashamed the uncle felt of the boy's appalling behaviour in the lecture room and the laboratory. He lamented how it grieved him to have to suffer the indignity of being recognized as a blood relation to the boy. Stinous would at first defend the boy against these moral onslaughts, wondering whether there wasn't perhaps an element of exaggeration in the uncle's accounts. Later, with a wry smile on his face, he would concede that the uncle had a point. The boy quickly realized that Stinous was on his side in this linguistic game. He was merely trying to humour the uncle and lower the temperature in his usual way. Nevertheless it was a mode of conversation that became boringly repetitive and, with its lack of novelty, soon deteriorated into total banality.

At the polytechnic the boy was finding it even harder to concentrate on his studies. His intermediate science course had become more lacking in interest for him than ever. He felt utterly frustrated by the sheer tedium of it all, and found the hardest part was trying to pretend that he was paying any attention whatever to the lecturer. He was simply not cut out to be an engineer. His aptitude for mathematics no longer gave him an edge when he was falling behind in everything else. The boy was in a quandary. He knew that going on with the engineering degree was a futile exercise and a waste of good money. If he was going to have to withdraw, then the sooner it happened the better.

All at once the decision was taken out of his hands. Without warning, the Israeli government put an embargo on the transfer of funds to foreign countries. The current term at the polytechnic was already paid for, but after that he would no longer be able to pay the tuition fees. It was a relief in one respect, though he also knew it was going to leave him without any means of support. Meanwhile, he could forget about attending lectures and concentrate on using the college's excellent recreational facilities. Two glorious months followed, in which, free as a bird, he made the best of the situation.

At this point another girl came into his life. She was a demure lass from the north of England, taking a course in domestic science. She had an attractive face and, the gang agreed, an alluring body. Her sex appeal arose from youthful innocence and freedom from artifice. Her lack of sophistication was as energizing as a breath of fresh air and all the gang fancied her, though none would make a move knowing the boy was taking an interest. For his part, he had been watching impatiently for an opportunity to satisfy the burning desire that was starting to consume him. Unless it could be dealt with it was threatening to destabilize him, and that was the last thing he needed in his present circumstances.

He took the plunge and invited her to a dance at the Hammersmith Palais. All of his friends were going to be there, especially his inner circle. That evening she was the belle of the ball. Wearing a charming dress, she looked lovely and bubbled with excitement. She was not exactly glamorous in the sense that glamour is understood today, but she seemed to generate an aura of warmth and fun around her. She was well aware that she was becoming the centre of attention; it gave her an added sparkle. She started to consume glass after glass of drink without keeping count. As the evening wore on, her movements began to show signs of unsteadiness. She swayed this way and that as if losing control of her body. As the last of her poise deserted her, she collapsed into the arms of the boy in what seemed to be a drunken stupor.

At this turn of events the boy felt let down and dismayed. She had promised to stay the night with him at Geraldine Road. He had been ecstatic at the prospect of a night of love with a girl he hardly knew, for the idea of intimacy with a stranger can titillate the mind as well as the senses. By his reckoning, the discovering of hidden qualities would bring for him a different kind of gratification. He persuaded himself that the evening might yet be saved. Bidding his friends good night, he left the dance hall, and half-steered, half-carried his companion to catch a trolleybus whose route from Hammersmith passed within a few yards of Geraldine Road.

As the journey proceeded she became very sick. Several times she threw up, drenching the boy with vomit. He could not hide his embarrassment from the other passengers, who fortunately were few at that time of night. At Geraldine Road he had to carry her upstairs to his bedroom on the top floor, and there, utterly exhausted, he deposited her unceremoniously on the bed. She remained virtually comatose as he undressed her gently, removing every garment with care, and for the first time uncovered her naked body. There was no arousal for him in the process as she remained semi-conscious and only stirred to be sick again. He was forced to spend the rest of the night playing nurse, cursing his luck for another adventure that had failed in its objective. His courtship of the girl from the north, that had held so much early promise, ended with her utter mortification in the morning, when she made a quick exit to avoid further embarrassment.

Although no physical bonding took place that night, their relationship survived the ordeal and briefly blossomed. The next time they met she was full of remorse and could not apologize enough for the fateful night when, through her sheer exuberance, she had drunk far too much and ruined the evening. She was honest enough to recognize that although her behaviour had been out of character its consequence had been to make her look cheap and dishevelled and perhaps give the boy the wrong signals about the kind of girl she was. In the event, all was forgiven, and matters resumed their natural course without ill-effects or recriminations.

Their time of togetherness, however, was brief. The girl moved on and took up with one of the boy's best friends. The pair became besotted with each other and were inseparable for several months, till that relationship also petered out. The novelty of the ingenuous girl from the north had finally evaporated. But its evaporation was slow. The delightful times she and the boy had spent together lingered on in his memory. It had been an uncomplicated relationship. Both had felt comfortable in a serendipitous sort of affair that was in no way stifling. He would continue to look back on the short period of their commitment with a deep affection unmarred by excessive passion or tempestuous episodes. It had all been a prelude to friendship rather than an enduring physical tie.

The feeling meanwhile began to grow among the trio of males at Geraldine Road that they were being held back by a common inability to take to the dance floor. In the case of the boy, he had never been taught as a child any of the social graces that could have helped him, as an adult, to blend in with a sophisticated world. His parents had frowned on anything that was not strictly within the parameters of an academic education, so he had never been taught a musical instrument or gone to dancing classes. As a result, he had missed out on many of the accomplishments that are considered by the modern world to be important social assets.

The problem was brought home to the uncle, Stinous and the boy whenever they found themselves out of place and isolated at social occasions where, as the band began to play, couples took to the dance floor and demonstrated their skills. After some discussion, it was decided they could overcome this social impediment by attending dance classes. Without further deliberation, they enrolled at a dancing school in the borough of Wandsworth. The classes were held in the evenings, and to begin with all three attended conscientiously. Slowly it became apparent to the boy that their fellow students were mostly middle-aged: old back numbers who had little else in their lives apart from this one night out a week. It was not something that troubled the uncle or Stinous in any way. They were that much older than the boy and perfectly at ease with the situation.

The uncle applied the methodical approach he used for everything to learning his dance steps. Stinous, being in some ways an extrovert, was more of a natural mover and tended to improvise, which made him a star pupil. The boy meanwhile experienced an innate awkwardness in translating the rhythms of the music to the movements of his feet. There was no incentive for him to give it a proper try. The chemistry was not working. If only there had been in the class a single young lady with some fire who might have persuaded him that he could do it. He looked around for any such young lady, but in vain. In the end he gave up, feeling the worse for the experience. Never again in his life did he venture on to a dance floor.

A diversion was brought about in Geraldine Road by the arrival of another guest. He was called Fouad and was a distant relation from the Holy Land. The boy had known him as a kid when they lived in the same neighbourhood of Haifa. Fouad had come to London for medical treatment for a condition that was causing his eyesight to fail. There was a real fear that he might eventually go blind. Fouad was an amiable character of medium build who never stopped laughing, despite his predicament. It was a contagious laugh, loud and resonant.

Fouad took over the boy's room, while the boy moved out to share with Stinous. For some reason he himself never understood, the boy, who liked Fouad a great deal, felt compelled to tease him whenever the whim drove him. There was no specific cause that triggered it off; simply a wild compulsion to get a rise out of him. The teasing escalated to torment. In the middle of the night the boy would get up and creep in on Fouad, who slept deeply, and tie him to the bedposts. To do this he used anything available, including shoe laces. Fouad would then wake with a jolt out of his heavy sleep and start screaming. This, in turn, roused the uncle, who slept in the room below and he would come rushing upstairs to untie him. The uncle would be frothing at the mouth with fury. He could hardly contain his anger. His complexion turned white and he shook uncontrollably. These extremes of rage were not at all in keeping with the image he displayed to the outside world. It was as if, all the time, there was a violent streak in him just dying for the chance to manifest itself, at least within the confines of the home.

The uncle would admonish the boy, shouting in his face that this was cruel and thuggish behaviour and pushing him roughly to one side. The protests of the boy, that he was merely having 'a bit of fun', as he termed it, just to keep Fouad on his toes, went to make matters far worse. The uncle was unable to appreciate the funny side of the situation. With his limited vision, he could only see things as black or white and could never settle on any of the intermediate shades; it had to be one or the other; there was no room for compromise. Fouad meanwhile took it all in his easy-going stride. It was as if he was immune to such silly games. When his medical treatment was over, he left with his sense of humour still intact.

In Maida Vale the Garnett family home continued to be a sanctuary for anyone in need of a good meal, or just of a cosy evening by the fire. All the circle of friends gathered there, and Julie, who was a bit of a tomboy at that time of her life, joined in any fun that was going. Peter Garnett would entertain them all with stories of his first encounters with the boy, telling how he had been dangled out of the window of a first-floor classroom at the polytechnic preparatory school. It had been done on the orders of the boy to teach him a lesson, though for what he had no idea. Afifi, when she heard this particular story, shrank in horror at such a callous disregard for the safety of her first-born son. She gave the boy a stern ticking off as he tried to deny the incident. Unfortunately the authenticity of Peter's account was verified by others at the gathering who had happened to witness it. Julie seemed secretly to admire the boy for the cheek of it all. She showed it clearly in her manner towards him. The boy found that part of her character to be most endearing.

The boy's life took a serious and dramatic turn as his money ran out. His student permit had also expired. When he went to the Home Office to ask that it be altered to allow him to seek employment, the request was refused. The condition could not be changed, he was told. He could no longer stay in the United Kingdom. Instead he must return to the country he had come from in the first place. The news came as a shattering blow. The boy could not imagine returning permanently to his country of origin, the land called Palestine, the land that had lost any hope of geographical or political statehood when it was subsumed within the state of Israel. Already it seemed like a foreign land. There was nothing there for him to go back for; no future in the region that he could envisage for himself. He felt completely assimilated with his new friends in England.

With what he felt to be his very survival at stake, he turned to Miss Newton. She saw at once the gravity of his predicament as he explained it, and summoned the help of George Hutchinson. These two powerful protectors then began to lobby for support for the boy's case among Members of Parliament. Notable among those to respond was the Conservative MP for the Isle of Ely, Major Edward Legge-Bourke, the author of regimental histories and books on military ceremony. Legge-Bourke in turn made a direct approach to Sir David Maxwell Fyfe, the formidable Home Secretary of the time.

Maxwell Fyfe had been Deputy Chief Prosecutor at the Nuremberg trials of Nazi war criminals after the war. He had broken down the defences of the wily Hermann Göring in cross-examination before the latter's suicide. His reputation was as a man who took a tough, unyielding line on matters where his mind was already made up. Yet there was an enlightened side to his principles. He had been a powerful advocate of the European Convention on Human Rights. Against the odds, he reconsidered the boy's case in the light of the pressure being applied in his favour. He relented, but with the proviso that the boy must only engage in unskilled labour. This was to ensure that no skilled jobs were taken away from British workers at a time when unemployment was high in the country. It was a triumph, but it came at a price. The boy would be allowed to stay, but only as long as he found work within the limits laid down. The Home Office could either veto or sanction any job he was offered.

It so happened that in the Midlands, in the manufacturing county town of Stafford, there lived a family friend called Gary Lovekin. The boy's family had got to know him when he was serving in the Palestine Police under the British Mandate. Mr Lovekin now held a senior management position in the English Electric Company. When he heard about the boy's difficulties, he contacted the Home Office to say he had a job available on the shop floor of the transformer division. He confirmed to the Home Office that this would be a job classified as 'unskilled'; it involved painting transformers and tightening nuts and bolts. He added that he had many jobs like it that he was unable to fill and would be grateful to the Home Office for any help they could give. The Home Office duly gave their approval for the boy's employment. It was another triumph, but again there was a downside.

The boy had a hollow feeling of dread mixed with disbelief at the prospect of wrenching himself away from London to live in a provincial industrial town somewhere to the north of Birmingham. The only person he knew there was Gary Lovekin. He had not even met Gary's wife, Betty. He was going to have to start afresh in an environment very different from anything he had known up till now. The questions kept coming into his mind. However was he going to slot in as part of a factory workforce? What would he have in common with men who had worked there all their lives? His only previous work experience had been his short time with Phillips Mills, the salvage company. The humdrum nature of that job, its mind-numbing monotony, had threatened his sanity after only a few days. Would this job in a factory setting affect him in the same way? Should he, after all, have gone home to Haifa and chanced his luck there? His mind grew clouded with doubts and he started to feel sorry for himself. Self-pity was not something that he had ever fallen prey to in the past. But now he felt vulnerable and brittle.

On the day before his departure from London, he did the rounds of all his friends and visited old haunts. As everyone wished him luck he vowed that he would return. In that era many houses still had no telephone; and where there was one, it was seldom used. The main way of keeping in touch was by post. The instant methods of communication taken for granted today did not exist. It was a very different world. People were content to wait for a letter, and glad when one arrived. He was resolved to be a regular correspondent, especially with his soulmate Julie.

The arrangement in Stafford was that the boy would lodge with the Lovekins for the first few weeks, until he found his feet. He was surprised to discover that their living accommodation was primitive in the extreme. It did not seem to tally remotely with Gary's senior management position at the English Electric factory. The house was small and dark and in a street of others just like it. It was cut off from the sun at all times, winter and summer. There was a strong, insistent smell of damp that permeated all one's clothing and seemed to penetrate one's bones. The accommodation was substandard and a threat to health, like that in which many thousands of others were living in Britain's as yet unreconstructed post-war world. It was the house in which Betty had been born; it had been the home of her family for generations, and had been left to weather the years as best it might. Nothing had been done to it in the way of maintenance or improvements.

There were two small bedrooms upstairs that were reached by a narrow staircase. On the ground floor there was a sitting-room, similarly cramped in its dimensions and in urgent need of redecoration. There was also a tiny kitchen equipped with worn utensils handed down from an earlier generation. Gary was a big man who moved about in these restricted quarters with difficulty, yet still somehow managed to negotiate the tight spaces without so much as a grumble. There was no bathroom. For ablutions the best that could be done was to take a bucket of water to whatever secluded corner could be found at any particular time. The situation's saving grace was that at least the lavatory was within the house and not outside in the yard, even if its plumbing had the same standard of antique dilapidation as the rest.

The Lovekins made an odd couple, from whichever way you viewed them. Gary was tall, and bulky in his upper torso, while Betty was small and slightly rounded. She was delicate and claimed to be suffering from bone cancer, but she seemed able to live a normal life in spite of this. Gary was very well informed. He worked hard, and he devoted any spare time that he had in the evenings to being an enthusiastic radio ham. On at least two occasions he was in communication with King Hussein of Jordan, who evidently shared the same hobby. Gary liked his beer, and he and his wife made regular visits to the local pub. Betty drank little, but was happy to keep her husband company. As the boy was their lodger and knew nobody in Stafford at that stage, they took him along to share their evenings out over pints of Worthington E. It was a brew he found rather potent. The upshot was that he slept heavily and had no time to reflect on his new life and its spartan conditions. There were times, however, when the strength of the beer went to his head, and on one or two occasions he even fell off his bike on the way home. He never was able to hold his alcohol well.

It took him about a quarter of an hour to cycle to the factory. He left the house to clock in at 8 a.m., returning home at about 6 p.m. During the winter months cycling could prove a nightmare. The roads were often icy and it was well before the time when there was clean-air legislation to counteract the ghastly problem of 'smog' in Britain's towns and cities. This thick sulphurous miasma was the result of uncontrolled levels of industrial pollution. In certain weather conditions the most dangerous time was during the evening journey home when, with visibility down to almost nil, things could become disorientating and frightening. Unable to see more than a foot or so ahead on the road, it was easy to lose one's sense of direction and a feeling of panic could set in. At such times the boy had to keep his nerve, which was not an easy task in the circumstances. Fortunately he managed to come to terms with this new hazard and a host of other difficulties that he encountered after leaving London and beginning his initiation into the hard realities of a working life.

The situation in the factory had also turned out to be hard to cope with. He was the only foreigner on the pay-roll. From the start his presence attracted mocking abuse of a sort outside his experience. Cat-calling was general, combined with remarks like, 'Where's your camel?' A few went so far as to call him a 'dirty Arab' to his face. For days he endured the insults and maltreatment, but the time came when he had put up with it enough. A notorious bully, who was used to throwing his weight about among his fellow workers, actually tried to manhandle him. The boy's reaction was swift and effective. He struck him so hard on the arm with a spanner that the man screamed with pain and had to undergo emergency treatment. The bully, however, refused to bring any charges against the boy and the incident was reported as an accident.

It was also a turning point. From that time on life changed positively for the boy. The abuse fell away as if by magic; his workmates took him under their wing; his popularity soared. As the months progressed, and by virtue of his cycling and the hard physical work involved in tightening nuts and bolts with a huge spanner all day, he developed strong muscles in every part of his body. He started flexing those muscles competitively, rising to challenges to see who could lift the greatest load. These trials of his new-found strength often resulted in torn ligaments in his arms and other minor injuries, but it was all done in good sport; somehow it enhanced the camaraderie of the workplace.

The boy began to feel more or less settled and started to look for more permanent accommodation. He did not want to overstay his welcome. Hospitable as the Lovekins were, his presence made their living space even more cramped and restrictive than it was at the best of times. It did not take him long to find alternative digs. He was offered a room by the Lowndes family in Peel Terrace. They had two very young daughters, and Stanley, the husband, worked in a footwear factory, shoe and boot manufacture being one of the traditional industries of Stafford. Joyce, his wife, had a job in a shop in the market-place. Joyce was the dominant partner in the marriage. She controlled every aspect of their domestic life. It was a situation Stanley accepted without a trace of resentment. When he came home on a Friday night with his pay packet, the first thing he did was hand it over to Joyce. She then counted out his spending allowance for the week.

In the same way that Monday was always washing day,

so in Stafford, and no doubt in many other industrial working-class centres, Friday was always bonking night. The pay packet was the key that ensured an easy entry. It was never the same during the week, when conjugal rights were not to be taken for granted. If a man needed to satisfy his sexual needs on other nights of the week, then he had to wheedle his way to gratification. The rights had to be earned. The boy never discovered whether this applied in the case of Stanley and Joyce. They gave every appearance of being a happily married couple who raised their children according to high moral principles.

On the shop floor the men used to talk about the sexual side of their lives at home with a raw openness that contrasted with the reticence of the British middle classes in these matters. After the incident with the spanner, as the boy came to be accepted on an equal footing with his fellow workers, he found himself being told more and more bedroom tales. They were often pathetic, and varied according to the personality involved. His closest workmate, with whom he shared a workbench, was always complaining that his wife hated sex to such a degree that he was allowed to touch her only twice a year. Even then, when she made the concession, she lay on her back almost motionless as she endured the torture, as she termed it, of being penetrated. She felt an utter disgust with the whole sexual act and would have preferred to banish it from her life. This morbid tale of sexual deprivation made the man's worker comrades indignant that he put up with it; they urged him to impose his rights as a husband – never mind the wife's abhorrence – and tried to taunt him into being a 'real man' with her.

A very different kettle of fish was the 'Joker', as everyone called him. He claimed to have the largest penis in the factory. If anyone wanted to put in a counter-claim, he would confidently declare, then let them prove it. No one took up the challenge and the Joker reigned supreme. He was a short rather squat fellow who, according to his own account, was rampant both outside and inside his marriage, but especially within it. He never ceased berating the boy's sex-starved workmate for his failure to dominate his selfish wife and letting down the male sex in general. Joker's own wife, it seemed, never tired of having sex at any time or in any position you could imagine. The secret, he advised, was to keep improvising and always aim for maximum penetration. He recalled how on one occasion, when his wife had been hoovering the sitting-room, dressed only in her knickers, he had crept up behind her, torn the knickers from her body and shagged her hard where she stood. She never even looked round to see who it was. When he had finished and she did look round, he gave her a sound slap for having, for all she knew, let a stranger take her from behind. Having told the tale, it was then necessary for him to dispel any notion that his wife might be promiscuous. In reality, he explained, she would have known who it was, because of the unmatched size of his penis. The reason for the slap was simple: 'to show her who was the man of the house'.

The boy settled in quite happily at his digs with the Lowndes family. British society had a long way to go yet in providing good standards of housing for its working people in the manufacturing towns and cities. As he had already seen during his stay with the Lovekins, they still lived for the most part in primitive conditions that had improved little since the death of Queen Victoria. The Lowndes's house also had no bathroom and the lavatory was located in a shed at the end of a small garden. During the night, in winter, you had to discipline your natural functions to avoid having to venture half-dressed out into the wind, rain or snow. There was no heating in the bedrooms and having to leave a warm bed was a real hardship. Before retiring to sleep, the boy had to put on thick flannel pyjamas with a vest underneath to protect himself from the dank coldness of the sheets before he plunged between them. It took him about ten minutes before he began to feel comfortable enough to be able to sleep. Managing to keep warm was a constant struggle. He could only fend off the cold by piling as many woollen blankets as he could find on top of the bed. Sometimes, if the weather was really severe, he would use a hot-water bottle. In those days, resorting to such an item was considered to be a sign of weakness. The spirit of the times demanded that you became hardened to everything.

Bathing arrangements were equally complicated and had to be precisely orchestrated in advance to enable all members of the household to take their turn. The ritual took place once a week on a Saturday, when a large galvanized bathtub was brought into the kitchen and placed in front of the kitchen range. The bath was then filled with hot water, an event looked upon as a moment of rare luxury. Once you had taken your bath, you felt fresh and clean, and confident about going out on a date. The feeling of well-being was short-lived, however. For the rest of the week you washed sparingly, for lack of more adequate facilities.

Wherever he went, the boy was always conscious of bodily smells among those he mixed with at work or in the street. The odours must have become a fact of life, but it surprised him that no one ever mentioned it or seemed repelled by it. He realized that he, too, must smell with the others, but perhaps the body became attuned to this lack of a full toilet regime; maybe it developed its own self-cleansing process as it strove to maintain a reasonable level of hygiene. The way society functioned under such begrimed conditions would have caused him revulsion if he had not found himself part of it. Cleanliness lay at the heart of civilization, and certain religious rites, including those of Islam, advocated the cleansing of the body with water before prayer. Later on in his life, he knew he could never survive without the basic facilities of a proper bath-room; in retrospect, he could not begin to explain how he had managed to lead a normal life when amenities of that kind were non-existent. It was mortifying to contemplate how there must have been a time when he had not only endured such indignity but had felt perfectly relaxed about it. In many households the Saturday-night bathwater tub was used to wash down every member of the family in turn, ending with the youngest child. At least at the Lowndes's the boy had been given water of his own.

One of the things that worried the boy when he set out from London for Stafford was how he would be able to cope with his sexual needs. How was he going to be able to satisfy them as a lone and rootless foreigner in what, he had been warned, was a small-town, inward-looking community? He realized that Stafford would certainly be very different from London. He was just going to have to improvise, making the most of any circumstances in which he found himself. And improvise is what he did.

The first girl to catch his attention worked behind the counter at the local chemist's shop. Hers was the beauty typified by Grace Kelly in the early 1950s: well-groomed with a distinguished look about her and fine cheekbones. So quintessential was her Englishness that she stood out in a crowd, presenting an image as fresh as morning dew. The boy was smitten the first time he saw her. When he went to the chemist to get a film developed, she served him with a smile that would have had a whole army prostrate at her feet. In the evening, alone in his room, he could think of nothing else except the girl in the chemist's shop. He began to fantasize about what might happen between them, and that night dreamed they were lovers. They were locked in a fierce embrace, and their naked bodies throbbed with such passion that he woke up, thoroughly aroused but unfulfilled. He lay in bed, tired and listless.

The dream recurred, with the same result, throughout the following week. The girl in the chemist's shop became his obsession, his object of desire. Her skin was like milk and her body could only have been shaped by divine intention. There was no way of banishing her from his mind, even if he so wished. He was trapped in an agony of lustful longing and had no way of taking command of the situation. He became lyrical about her and could only describe her in poetic terms. Eventually he plucked up the courage to ask her out. She was hesitant but curious. In the end her curiosity overcame her hesitation.

They had something to eat in a café before going on to a movie. In the cinema they sat in the back row. The boy got no further than holding her hand. There was an initial resistance before she began to warm to his affectionate advances. Afterwards he saw her home. On the next date she became more responsive, but still remained very much in control of her emotions. She was flattered by the attention, for she was only eighteen, though at the time he did not realize she was so young. She was also apprehensive about where all this might be leading. As yet she had had no real sexual experience, she confessed. She could only give herself without reservation to the man who would become her husband. The boy had no choice but to recognize that she had been brought up to have moral convictions he must respect. It did not follow that purity meant total prohibition. Sometimes it could awaken the very opposite. In any case, the boy was reluctant to give up, despite being aware that such sincere principles should not be disregarded.

He continued to pursue her and their relationship reached the point where they pleasured each other without engaging in intercourse. The boy was always elated after each petting session, though the ultimate fusion of their bodies was still out of the question. After two months of this, both of them realized they were coming to a dead end; that if they went on it was all likely to finish in heartbreak and acrimony. They ceased seeing each other, but the boy was never to forget the wonderful girl who had served him in the chemist's shop and become a dream that never was. It was a memory to cherish: the English rose he had so desperately wanted to pluck but who had somehow eluded his grasp.

The next romantic episode in his life was a very different matter. Angelina was about twenty-one, a girl of Greek extraction who sang occasionally with the local band at concerts in the town hall. Every hot-blooded young male in town had designs on her, and she knew it. When the boy's workmates at the factory spoke about Angelina, they slipped into rhapsodic mode. They dared the boy to try and get a date with her. It was a challenge he could not resist. The next time she was due to sing at the town hall he booked himself a ticket and went along to listen. When she launched into a medley of some of Doris Day's greatest hits, he was enchanted by the way she interpreted them. After the band had played their last piece, he approached her and was surprised at the immediate rapport there seemed to be between them. Their lives were to become linked together for the next twelve months.

The boy had got to know the Lovekins well during his time with them, and after he moved out he continued to see them often. Gary, in particular, grew into a loyal, dependable friend. Betty was more problematic. Although he had a great fondness for her, the boy had begun to see through her subterfuges as she feigned all kinds of physical ailments to make sure she held centre stage. One of her ploys was to keel over as if in a fainting fit. These moments were cleverly staged so that her chosen victim would have to pick her up and revive her, displaying a close concern. In most cases, at this time, the victim was the boy. He was incapable of showing her anything but kindness, and in return she began to buy him gifts. What she really wanted from him remained unclear, and he was reluctant to find out. Any hint of a romantic attachment would have put at risk his friendship with Gary, to whom he owed so much. The boy found himself walking a tightrope to avoid falling into an unthinkable entanglement. Betty was basically superficial and a very jealous woman, and the fact that the boy's focus of attention was on someone else caused her much displeasure and a degree of resentment.

Matters came to a head when Gary offered the boy a set of keys to their new home. The new house was modern and spacious and had all the up-to-date facilities that the old one lacked, including a telephone. Gary told the boy that he could come there to take a bath, or if he and Betty were out for the evening, to bring a girlfriend back to entertain her. There was no way the boy could have taken a girl to the Lowndes's house in Peel Terrace, where the lack of space and the presence of the little daughters would have made privacy impossible. Betty certainly had no objections to the boy taking a bath in her new home; in fact she welcomed it. The boy sensed, however, that she would have found the idea of him taking a girl back there quite intolerable

By now Angelina and the boy were established as an item, though they lived apart. They had been making love wherever they could: in doorways, down dark alleyways, even in snow patches during the winter months. They used their overcoats to shield their wriggling bodies from the snow and the frosty air. It was a foolish way to carry on. The boy was starting to suffer from backache, stiffening knees and symptoms of rheumatism; the health of both of them was being undermined by their open-air recreation. With the harsh rigours of winter thus playing havoc with their amorous activities, the offer of the house keys by Gary held out the prospect of a promised land such as had sustained the Israelites during their wanderings in the desert after they escaped out of Egypt. The young couple too had now found their refuge, though one of a different sort. At last their wanderings were over – or so they briefly thought.

With Gary's connivance, the boy devised a strategy whereby he and Angelina could sneak into the house when the Lovekins were out for an evening – the idea being that Betty need never find out. The arrangement lasted until she did, and then all hell broke loose. Nothing would placate Betty. The sanctuary that the boy and Angelina had found for themselves was denied to them for ever. Betty tried to justify the stand she was making against having her house used for 'immoral purposes', as she put it. It was because she had the boy's best interests at heart, she said, and she was duty bound to feel a sense of responsibility towards him. It was all humbug, of course. Even she must have realized that her protestations of concern carried no real credibility. The truth was that she was incensed at the idea that the boy was having a sexual relationship with Angelina; she could not stand the thought of it. She was extremely jealous, without ever admitting the fact to herself.

As is usual in such cases, there was a sadness in the background. Betty had been born an only child and craved attention. She had visions of becoming a television personality, and many years later she did appear on local television, talking about cosmetics, for at one stage she owned and ran a hairdressing salon. Her life with Gary was a lonely one. He was either preoccupied with his work at the factory or tinkering away with his radio transmitter. Gary had no time for chit-chat with her, and she sought that kind of social comfort elsewhere. Her sexuality defied classification and remained a puzzle. It seemed to be not so much a matter of frustrated physical desires as some sort of cry for help. Her marriage had done nothing to aid her in fulfilling her ambitions or propelling her into a more elevated social stratum. She constantly sought the reassurance that she was an attractive woman with striking sex appeal, one who ranked high in men's estimation and who was still as desirable as ever. Betty had a generous side to her nature, but when all was said and done she was morbidly self-absorbed.

The boy's relationship with Angelina meanwhile went through its ups and downs. She began to want more of a show of commitment from him. It was something he did not feel able to give. He could not see his time in Stafford as being more than a transitional period, a pragmatic necessity from which he must move on as soon as the time was right. To do this he was going to have to keep his options open. It was clear that there could be no long-term future for him in a provincial industrial town like Stafford. He must be ready to make a positive, definite move the minute he saw an opportunity.

His escape route, when it came, was an unlikely one. He was offered the chance to work in the south-east of England as a steeplejack. The idea of heights scared him stiff, but he readily accepted the job. It no longer seemed to matter to him what he did, so long as he was doing something different. He needed a change, both of direction and environment. Moreover, the move was going to take him back to within reach of London.

Leaving Stafford turned out to be an emotional affair. His workmates at the factory were very supportive and had tears in their eyes as they said goodbye and wished him well. The Lowndes and the Lovekins were equally sorry to see him go, but they understood that his destiny lay elsewhere. The break with Angelina was the most painful part. They had been together for more than a year and were deeply fond of each other, despite the fact that their relationship was inclined to be tempestuous at times. They agreed they would remain friends. Angelina said she would write to him in London. They might yet, she speculated, spend the rest of their lives together if the Good Lord ordained it. It was a touching thought, but the boy had to be honest with himself. He could see no future in it, however sincere he knew his love to be.

But no amount of rationalizing assuaged the hurt of having to leave her to seek out new pastures. In life we often recognize the futility of our circumstances, yet still we cling to them for fear of *terra incognita*. We embrace whatever bitter comforts we have at a given time, in the full knowledge that their continuance is doomed. We shy away from making difficult decisions in the hope that time will resolve them for us. The boy agonized over his separation from Angelina, but it was wiser to make a clean break there and then and bear the consequences than wait for contrary emotions to take over in time and sour the whole relationship. At the same time it was far better, he thought, to have loved and suffered than to have missed such a profound experience of human intimacy altogether.

The boy's life as a steeplejack, working on power pylons for the Central Electricity Board, kept him always literally on the edge. He would wake in the night, trembling with fear. Because of an obsessive concern for his safety, his family, in all his years of growing up in Palestine, had gone to the utmost lengths to protect him from physical harm. Now he had no way of knowing what dangers awaited him when he went to work each morning. Would this be the day that he fell to his death? Would he survive to get home safely one more evening? He could take it only a day at a time.

He had found himself lodgings in Flood Street, Chelsea. The room was small, dark and airless. Its one window overlooked a courtyard that caught no direct sunlight. Cooking facilities in the room were utterly basic, consisting of a single gas ring, which was hardly adequate for preparing a reasonable meal. For all the lodgers there was only one lavatory and bathroom, but as he rose to shave at 5 a.m., long before any of the others were awake, he normally had it to himself. Sustained by a diet of Weetabix and milky coffee for breakfast, he then set out to catch an early commuter train from Victoria Station to wherever the day's assignment happened to be. He had to report for work at 9 a.m.

His first day on the job was an experience that has remained for ever vividly imprinted on his mind. He had to climb with the men to the highest point of a pylon to help with replacing faulty ceramic insulation pots. His new-found workmates lost no time in telling him how one of their number, the day before, had fallen as he tried to negotiate a steel girder on his way up. The weather was wet and windy, and the man must have slipped. Fortunately his fall happened in the early stages of his ascent, before he had reached a height from which a drop could have been fatal. He had been taken to hospital to be treated for concussion, but had suffered no permanent injury.

Like the others, the boy had to wear a leather safety belt that could be anchored to a bar when it was necessary to lean backwards and have both hands free to work with. Yet although the safety belt was totally reliable, he was never able to free himself from the habit of still holding on with one hand, even when the belt was hooked in place. He needed that double assurance however much it restricted his freedom of movement. Despite being constantly reprimanded, he was quite unable to let go and hang freely. The thought of entrusting his life to a leather belt simply made him too afraid. It was a sign he would never make the grade as a true and seasoned steeplejack.

The older men were very protective of the boy. They made sure he was never exposed to any unnecessary risks. They realized he was not cut out for this sort of work and sympathized with the circumstances that had impelled him to join them in their perilous occupation. If the location of a job was too far out from London to make commuting practicable, then 'the boys', as the members of the work gang called themselves, would usually stay at a bed-and-breakfast lodging. The work for the Electricity Board was well paid and included danger money. Even so, the boys would sometimes decide all to bed down together in the same room to save expense. The boy found this experience of communal rooming alien at first, but as with so much else that had happened to him, it was a matter of making the effort to adapt.

The local pub was always the steeplejacks' place of refuge. They drank beer mostly, played darts, told each other dirty jokes or fantasized about women, perhaps a shade crudely. If they got on to politics, they generally blamed the upper classes for keeping the working classes down. There was no malice or rancour in anything they said. It was nothing more than the usual bar-room polemics of the sort that seldom make much sense, at whatever level they are exercised, but enliven the atmosphere and raise voices an octave or two higher than usual. The boy, as he mixed with them, found their honesty and way of life intriguing. They lived for the day and asked no favours of any man. He saw from their example how danger as an occupational hazard had to be looked on with a nonchalant, matter-of fact attitude, otherwise life would become intolerable. Luck and bad omens played no part in their profession. They lived literally with their lives on the line and seemed to relish weighing the odds between life and death as if they were engaged in a poker game. Their sense of humour bordered on the black side; they rarely discussed or even acknowledged the dangers, since this would destabilize the daily routine and be bad for morale.

The boy enjoyed the company of these men who had chosen such a risky and dangerous job, scaling power pylons and working in the direct vicinity of cables carrying

120,000 volts. If it rained, it added to the hazards. They had to be particularly careful not to get too close to the cables, water being a deadly conductor of electricity. The combination of height and high voltage became especially lethal in a downpour of rain or a sudden squall. It made you feel as if you were trapped in an electric storm in the space around you. If bad conditions threatened, the site had to be abandoned very quickly before panic had time to set in. The downward descent needed to be negotiated with extra care for fear of missing a foothold and tumbling on to the hard concrete base below.

Heroics and bravado counted for little in this line of work. Caution and concentration were more likely to keep you alive. The boy saw how, perversely, there are many attractions to danger, how men seemed drawn to a life on the edge of the void. The macho image was often a factor, but it seemed the real motivation was to challenge the fear of death that all men carry in the deepest recesses of their souls; to challenge it by facing it head-on. The taste for danger was virtually addictive. The adrenaline surge was like the release of a potent drug which drove men forward in directions that needed strict control. Unchecked, their excessive zeal was certain to become a gratuitous threat to life.

Having to climb with the men and work with them in the danger zone brought with it a real appreciation of that fear: a fear that numbed the boy's senses and almost reduced him to a vegetable. The only comparable moment in his life had been when he first came to England through raging seas on the cross-channel ferry in 1949. Memories of both these ordeals became indelible.

The social life that he had hoped to renew with the move back to London, meanwhile, proved to be non-existent. He was too exhausted to go out in the evenings, and so remained a total celibate during the three months that he stuck with the job of steeplejack. He could not have afforded the time to devote to a girlfriend, even had one been readily available. It was like being in a desert with no oasis in sight. His entire bank of energy was used up in the effort to survive. He decided that his nerve was going to go completely unless he could change to work where he could at least keep his feet on the ground. The Home Office agreed to the boy being allowed to look for something less hazardous. When a vacancy for a porter at the Elizabeth Garrett Anderson Hospital, near Kings Cross, came to his attention, he applied. He also found alternative lodgings in Chelsea – a room in Sydney Street.

Elizabeth Garrett Anderson had been the first woman to qualify as a medical doctor in Britain and she founded the hospital, originally a dispensary for women, in 1866. The establishment was meant for women and was staffed entirely by women, except for the portering staff, who were exclusively male. There was a common room where the porters could sit, and here they would stay, waiting to be dispatched to one part of the hospital or another when a suitable job needed doing. The tasks they were called on to deal with included collecting rubbish or waste, wheeling patients between departments and removing dead bodies from the ward to the mortuary.

There were occasions when a summons came for a porter to go to the operating theatre to lug heavy equipment about. If this happened, the man was required to gown up in the same outfit as theatre staff and surgeons and observe the same rigorous hygiene precautions to ensure a bacteria-free area around any patient on the operating table. Mondays were the days for women to attend as out-patients for minor gynaecological surgery. Although they were put to sleep with anaesthetic for any surgical procedure, they were expected to go home again by evening. On Mondays the boy was often asked to attend the theatre in his porter capacity, to stand by in case of an emergency. It was an odd situation for him to occupy in an all-female establishment. He was completely untrained in medical matters, yet found himself witnessing the laying bare of women's intimate parts on a regular basis. It was as if he became a pair of eyes that was expected to see nothing, though it was impossible for him to ignore the activity that formed the centre of attention in the operating theatre. His own affinity with the female anatomy suffered a minor setback after the shock of observing the technique used for stretching the vagina in a woman where the passage had been too tight to allow proper examination.

The effects of this did not last long, however. He was leaving home at 6 a.m. each morning to catch the first tube that ran from South Kensington to Kings Cross and starting his day at the hospital by having breakfast with a host of foreign maids. He was soon making up for his months of celibacy when working on the power lines. Suddenly it was bonanza time. He could select from among the girls for various dates in the evenings and was spoilt for choice. He was back in his element and thanked the benevolent Lord for his good fortune. Not only had he survived the traumas of his steeplejack days, but here he was, landed in the most enviable situation of being looked after both physically and emotionally by a bevy of young women with whom he had a great deal in common. They, too, were having to cope with personal difficulties as they strove to preserve their sense of identity while working in the hospital. The work they did was not so much out of choice as out of necessity, so they could learn English and familiarize themselves with a new environment in a strange country. Their future was as uncertain as his, and the common factor between them was a determination to make a better life for themselves. The boy's dreams and those of the girls coincided, with the result that they gave each other encouragement and enjoyed a serenity in each other's company that was hard to define.

Then there was more good news. When he came to make his application to have his annual residency permit renewed, he was told by the Home Office that he no longer needed to observe the original restriction. He was being accorded permanent residency in the United Kingdom and could seek any job he wished. The dream of better days in store was beginning to come true. But first, he felt, he needed a change of scenery. He consulted with his university friend, Adam Rudzki, and they began to make plans for a hitchhiking trip from Paris to the Côte d'Azur in the South of France and onwards to Corsica.

They took the cross-channel ferry and the train to Paris. Once in Paris, they spent a few days staying in cheap hotels before heading out for Versailles, from where they planned to begin their hitchhiking adventure by getting a lift to Marseille. They managed to hitch a lift on the back of a lorry that took them as far as Fontainebleau, and there their luck deserted them. As they tramped along the highway it seemed that every car they hailed deliberately ignored them. After a while they grew tired and frustrated, till their spirits were lifted by the sight of two pretty young girl hitchhikers sitting on the grass at the roadside. The sneaking thought occurred to them that perhaps they could use them as bait to get a lift.

The girls seemed quite young and very knowing, like two Lolitas. Dressed in skimpy blouses and baggy short shorts, they exuded sex appeal. The shorts put the maximum emphasis on their slinky legs, which as they sat they kept strategically parted to give a tantalizing view of their inner thighs, and even a fleeting glimpse of scanty transparent knickers, which concealed hardly anything. The boy and Adam were astounded by the sheer nerve of it, and the boy could not resist getting out his camera to take a photo. Gallingly, before they could approach them to suggest a team effort, the first car to come along stopped and the girls nonchalantly got to their feet, stepped aboard and were whisked away. It was a bull's-eye at the first attempt. The boy and Adam, somewhat crestfallen, continued walking till evening, when Adam suggested they had better sleep in the woods. The boy was vehement he would do no such thing, so instead they headed for a local youth hostel and spent the night there. The next morning they decided to cut their losses and catch a train to Marseille, even though it meant they would no longer have funds to get as far as Corsica.

On arrival in Marseille they installed themselves in

another youth hostel, in what had once been an old school. It made rough accommodation, but that did not matter a great deal in the intense heat of July. They toured the city and crossed the bay to visit the château d'If, the former fortress prison from which the comte de Monte-Cristo made his dramatic escape, disguised as a corpse sewn up in a sack, in Alexandre Dumas *père*'s great romantic novel. Leaving Marseille, they took a bus eastwards along the French coast to the town of Le Lavandou. As they paused there, they heard about a nudist colony called Heliopolis on the Île du Levant, which lay a few miles offshore, out in the Mediterranean. It seemed to them that this might provide another intriguing diversion. The island was in part taken up by the naturist enclave, while the rest was given over to some government agency for experimental purposes to do with the military. The Île du Levant was accessible by regular ferry service, but it was too late to catch a boat that day. Rather than spend their dwindling resources on a hotel, they decided to sleep out on the beach. The night was long and the air became chilled. They could hardly wait to see the sun rise and feel its warmth.

The first ferry next morning carried them to the island, where the inhabitants of the small port town earned a living by catering for the needs of the many visitors who came to the island from far and wide in search of nature and the natural in every sense. Even the shop assistants served the customers naked, except for a fig leaf to cover their private parts. At first the boy and Adam found it a bizarre experience to go into a bakery and see a woman dangling her breasts among the freshly baked loaves she was handling. Did the bread taste better as a result, they wondered. As the initial weirdness of the experience began to wear off, they made their way to the top of a mountain where there was a youth hostel and encampment. Here various formalities had to be gone through, including the need to register themselves as youth members of the cult of naturism. Then they were each allocated a place in one of the tents and requested to go about naked like everyone else.

Nervously they removed their clothing and braced themselves to face the ordeal of making a grand entrance at the main compound where the community gathered. It was only to be expected that they would briefly become the focus of attention. For one thing, new merchandise always attracts till the novelty wears off; for another, their bodies were white in contrast to the glowing browns of those whose skin had been exposed to the sun's rays for a long period. There was also no escaping the curiosity humans always feel for seeing those parts of other people's bodies that are normally concealed. As soon as the assembled company had looked their fill, the boy and his friend Adam blended into the landscape.

The youth club which the boy and Adam had joined consisted of dedicated followers of the French writer and philosopher Jean-Paul Sartre. The boy was very familiar with his work and considered himself a faithful disciple. Existentialism had an exciting appeal for young people in those days, with its emphasis on man's needing to define his place in the world in which he found himself by drawing on his own mental resources and his own human experience, God (or the idea of God) having departed the scene. Among Sartre's writings, he had read the novels *La*

Nausée and the trilogy *Les Chemins de la liberté*, as well as some of the plays, notably *Les Mouches* and *La Putain respecteuse*. He therefore felt completely at home in the intellectual ethos of the youth camp, though other aspects of the collective experience needed a degree of adjustment. There were no showers or running water. The only toilet facilities were communal and consisted of a large hole in the ground in the woods. It was the ultimate exercise in social levelling. You would be squatting to relieve yourself over the hole when somebody else came to squat next to you and do the same. Their presence had an inhibiting effect on the uninitiated through embarrassment. The anal sphincter would tighten and the natural function seize.

Their main diet in camp was bread and cheese washed down with quantities of cheap wine. They also bought fruit, vegetables and tinned sardines at the shop. They could not afford sun-tan lotion, so to protect their skin they used olive oil, which had some rather unfortunate results. There were times in the evenings, after everyone had eaten and before merriment took over, when the general talk turned into animated discussions and heated arguments over the true meaning of existentialism; what it stood for and its various interpretations. At such moments the atmosphere began to sizzle with intellectual fervour. The shedding of inhibitions and exposing of the body in nakedness became all of a piece with the baring of the soul. It was an invigorating experience that the boy recognized as a unique coming together of circumstances, time and place. He drank in every part of it eagerly; he would never encounter anything like it again.

As the arguments petered out, the desire for enter-tainment took over. Musical talents came to the fore and there was a lot of dancing before the day's activities were rounded off with games sessions. One notable contest involved two people sitting opposite each other astride a wobbly bench, their feet not touching the ground. While each of them used one hand to ward off blows to their own head, with the other they dealt blows about the other's head with enough force to make them topple off. Whoever remained on their perch at the end of the contest was declared the winner. Late at night the *mistral* started to blow down the Rhône Valley and the tents in which the revellers slept began to sway as if keeping time with the wind. The camp beds inside the tents were arranged almost touching because of the limitations on space, and there was no segregation of the sexes.

The whole business of nakedness had made the boy and his friend apprehensive about how their own bodies would respond to seeing naked women all around them. Could they resist getting erections? If they failed to repress the urge, would they find themselves the embarrassed subjects of mocking hilarity among their comrades? The odd thing was that with so much flesh on show in such a natural, matter-of-fact way, the erotic mystery seemed to vanish. During the day, they spent their time on the beach, where the whole colony gathered in the burning sun. There they saw all sizes and shapes of naked bodies. Some were young, some old, some very old. They witnessed the beauty of the human form alongside the ugly and grotesque. The widely diverse sunbathers presented a living frieze that included the gorgeous and the repellent. Some private parts in either sex could be threatening or disturbing to look at; others were more benign. In the final analysis, allure and revulsion walked hand in hand: beauty is truly in the eye of the beholder. They could hardly have had a better demonstration of the fact, and they took the lesson on board. It was forbidden to photograph any of the naked women, but that did not prevent them trying it on surreptitiously. The only occasion on which cameras were openly allowed was on the night of the Nude Miss Île du Levant contest, when the gorgeous winner could be photographed naked.

With their time on the island at an end, the boy and Adam decided to vary their return route to the French mainland and take a boat to Hyères, which was farther along the road to Nice. It was about a three-hour journey, and as luck would have it a strong wind got up and whipped the waves into a ferment. Everyone on board – even the skipper's young mate – was seasick, except for the old skipper himself. He kept one hand on the wheel to steer against the waves and in the other clutched an opened bottle of red wine, from which he refreshed himself at regular intervals. The boy suffered from terrible nausea, but even when the ordeal was at its worst, he had to admit it was nothing compared with his channel crossing in 1949. They arrived in Hyères at about noon and bought some lemons to suck to settle their stomachs as they went to sit on a bench in the town square to recover.

The week they had spent on the Île du Levant was an adventure they would not have forgone. Nakedness does not in itself arouse sexual desire; there are times when it discourages it. The libido is stimulated by mysterious impulses that spring from a longing to unravel something tantalizingly hidden. Some of the women they had seen were stunningly attractive, yet they had felt no physical response. It only went to prove how it was concealment that strengthened desire through the power of imagination. The point was illustrated after they had arrived in Hyères and were making their way along a rather windy quayside. A gust of breeze caught the skirt of a curvaceous young woman who happened to be walking on the sea front. The glimpse they had of her knickers was enough to make the blood of the boy and his friend tingle with excitement. They were back in the real world.

Apart from heading from Hyères along the coast to Nice, and an encounter with a couple of stray women that led to some much needed sexual release, little more happened before they returned by train to Paris. Back in the capital, they managed to find the cheapest possible little hotel, just off place St-Michel, but after two or three days had to face the fact that they could afford to eat nothing but tomatoes and bread as they sat on the banks of the Seine. It was time to go home. The boy needed to turn to the serious contemplation of his future. He had nowhere to live in London. Before embarking for the Continent, he had given up his room in Sydney Street and put his few belongings into store. Adam, who was finishing a degree in aeronautics, had to board outside London during the week as commuting would have involved too much travel. He therefore suggested to the boy that he move in with his mother, who had a house in Acton. He would be able to stay there rent free in return for keeping an eye on his mother, Mrs Rudzka, who suffered from a heart murmur. It was an offer the boy felt he could not afford to refuse. He had no money, and the prospect of being able to live very cheaply naturally had its appeal. However, it would still be two months before he could take up Adam's offer. He had a temporary job lined up in the meantime – as a bouncer in a Soho nightclub.

The job as a bouncer had been offered by the nightclub's proprietor, a former Oxford graduate who had been through a stretch in prison for a drug offence involving cannabis. He and the boy had formed a kind of friendship. The boy was asked to act as a personal bodyguard as well as a bouncer. His duties would not begin until after 2 a.m.; the first part of the night was taken up with the club's function as a jazz club.

The club premises were situated on the second floor of a dilapidated building down an alley off Charing Cross Road, directly opposite the famous Foyle's bookshop. It was the sort of joint you would be more likely to come across in the Bowery district of New York, though it was perhaps less seedy and certainly not in such a dangerous neighbourhood. The jazz played was mostly in the New Orleans revival style; the so-called 'trad fad' was taking off in Britain among many young, up-and-coming popular musicians. Skiffle – the poor man's music using washboards – was already an influence and would soon turn into a profitable craze for the music business.

The boy was a jazz novice in so far as it was a kind of music completely new to him. He responded to it instantly and found himself caught up by its insistent, powerful swinging rhythms and the improvised melodic lines of trumpet, saxophone, clarinet or piano soaring above the base. He thrilled to the more elegiac numbers based on the twelve-bar blues, where the fall of the melody seemed to contain all the sorrow of an enslaved race over two hundred years of suffering. There was sadness on the one hand, but on the other an unquenchable resilience and capacity for human joy. It was music he could relate to. The club's patrons were mostly committed jazz enthusiasts who appreciated and revelled in the intensely charged atmosphere. During its brief life, the club became well known for the quality and brilliance of its players – some already famous and on their way to international stardom. With gigs from such established figures as Chris Barber and Ken Colyer, it attracted a class of musician keen to find a testing ground in which to improve their skills and try out their music in front of a live audience.

The boy was often joined by his friend Adam, who came to hear the jam sessions at the club. Many of the Soho landmarks were well known to them. Some they visited for pleasure; others out of sheer necessity. In particular there was Chiquito's, a coffee house in Hanway Street, off Tottenham Court Road. With its bohemian, easy-going policy, its unpretentious and friendly atmosphere, it virtually fulfilled the role of a dating agency without intending to be one. The boy became particularly well known there as he used to hold court at one of its tables in the afternoons and early evenings before going to work, usually in the company of women. It became a second home. Another favourite haunt was the pub adjoining the Dominion Theatre on the corner of Tottenham Court

Road and New Oxford Street, where Adam and the boy could sample a variety of barley wines, very strong brews in small bottles. They often entertained their friends in the pub, and occasionally held a binge there if they had something special to celebrate. Another establishment they frequented was the all-night branch of Boots in Piccadilly Circus, open twenty-four hours a day for anyone needing medication or an emergency prescription. Their visits to it were usually late at night for a spoonful of kaolin mixture, consisting of china clay with a touch of morphine, to settle a sick stomach. The boy's appearances at the dispensary were so regular that the pharmacist had his dose of kaolin ready whenever he saw him approaching.

The two friends were also often to be seen in one or other of the two delis in Great Windmill Street, munching away on rye-bread sandwiches of warm salt beef with lashings of mustard and large pickled cucumbers on the side. This was a culinary treat to which they always looked forward. There was also Henneky's cider bar in Kingly Street, where they drank large quantities of cider simply because it was cheaper than beer and probably quite as effective. At the weekends Adam drove about town in a 1934 Alvis, a car that had style and character, though its radiator was forever boiling over. They needed to travel with a spare gallon of water aboard to ensure they reached their destination without major mishap. It was a matter of living in the fast lane with a slow motor; contending with modern traffic in a period vehicle was as difficult as it was colourful.

The boy's duties as a bouncer had its bad moments as well as its perks. That in the job he would sustain various minor injuries was only to be expected. There was one incident, however, which could have had serious consequences. A burly Scotsman, who had been drinking heavily, became obstreperous and threatened to cause a major disruption in the club. The boy, when he went to eject him, found himself on the receiving end of a well crafted blow, delivered with deadly precision, that sent him tumbling down two flights of stairs. He was quite badly hurt and shocked and had to be taken to the Charing Cross Hospital, then still at its old address in the Charing Cross district, to be given casualty treatment. His back was injured and he had bruises on both legs. From this he drew a useful lesson: never underestimate an opponent, not even one who appears totally uncoordinated and off-guard with inebriation. The boy had dropped his guard when he tried to throw out the Scotsman and paid a heavy price for one moment of inattention.

At a later stage of his life, after he was married, he needed to attend the Charing Cross Hospital as an out-patient for a minor swelling of the thumb. To his utter surprise, the hospital register recorded the number of times he had attended for treatment in his former rackety existence as a jazz-club bouncer. Although he was embarrassed when the nurse mentioned how well known his name was for his regular visits during that period, he also felt a kind of nostalgia for those days that he could hardly conceal. He remembered how most nights, after the band had packed up and gone and the club had been closed, the proprietor would lead the way to Archer Street, on the southern edge of Soho. The reason for going there was to pick up what was usually a small packet of cannabis to see them through the small hours. An old barber's shop in the same street was where, during the day, they would go to shop for their French letters (as condoms were called in those days).

Sex was constantly in the air in Soho in one form or another. Not many steps round the corner in Great Windmill Street was the famous Windmill Theatre, where the Van Damm management had had its 'revuedeville', a form of non-stop variety, running since 1932. Even during the worst of the London blitz it had kept going. The proud slogan, 'We never closed', should have been, wags of theatreland always joked, 'We never clothed.' The Lord Chamberlain's rules of censorship decreed that if there was nudity on stage, then there must be no movement. Revuedeville featured *tableaux* of nude girls in frozen classical poses interspersed with other entertainment, including the acts of young comedians like Michael Bentine or Tony Hancock learning their craft in difficult circumstances. There was no doubting what the customers, mainly male, had queued up round the block to see.

From Archer Street the boy and the proprietor would then head off into the Soho jungle to track down some weird party or other, news of which had been picked up on the grapevine. Soho at the time had a sort of lurid sleaziness that has completely gone from it today. It formed the underbelly of a sin-conscious Britain, where all that was forbidden could be obtained at a price. Streetwalkers lurked unambiguously in doorways and on corners, waiting for men to make an approach as they cruised in what would today be called a 'tolerance zone'. The area was popular with poets and artists, who were drawn to the raffish pubs and drinking clubs, and with East End gangsters, like the Kray brothers, who made it their stamping ground when they were 'up West', as well as with all sorts of other characters from the fringes of society. The police, it was said, were tolerant of many of the dubious aspects of this twilight world since for them it was a valuable source of information on underworld activities. The continental food shops, some of which had been run by the same family over several generations, gave an added un-English *frisson* in a Britain not yet used to eating garlic, and imported exotic vegetables like aubergines from the Continent.

As a hub of prostitution, Soho was given a certain lurid local colour by its professional ladies before the Street Offences Act was brought in to try to make them less visible. Women of varying ages loitered on street corners near Shaftesbury Avenue, looking to pick up clients. A way they had of operating was in black cabs. One night, back in the days when they were students together at the Battersea Polytechnic, Adam and the boy, neither of whom had ever been with a prostitute, dared each other to go up to Soho and sample the experience. Both were very nervous, but they managed to pluck up courage and approached two young women, who at once hailed a taxi conveniently parked near by. Into the taxi they piled as a foursome and the cab went speeding around the West End until the job was done. It was all over in a matter of minutes. The girls orchestrated the action with mechanical precision, hitching up their skirts and unbuttoning the men's trousers. For the cab driver, it was a familiar routine, with no erotic connotations whatsoever. For Adam and the boy, it proved an ungratifying and sordid experiment that was certainly not worth the effort and expenditure.

As the boy continued to gain insights into the idio-syncrasies of British society at different levels, one of the observations he made was of the male tendency in its upper echelons to use prostitutes. Aristocrats and celebrities, especially if they came from a public-school background, were often drawn down, it seemed, into the lower depths of depravity. It was not so much that their women folk denied them the sexual gratification they needed, but more because they felt wary of commitment and an urge to rebel against an element of puritanism in their early upbringing. A prostitute offers her services and gets paid. The balance in the transaction is simple. It requires no after-service, whereas relationships that lead to sex are complex and carry warning signs for a lot of these men. Another aspect is that consorting with a prostitute allows inhibitions to be easily discarded in her company, whereas in real life we are programmed to follow conventions that restrict our patterns of behaviour. Being able to act as oneself is perhaps one attraction that lures men to seek women who give them what they want without fear of repercussion. Another may be the loss of identity, since neither par-ticipant is required to offer anything that is not relevant to the task. It is sex in the raw without embellishment or any of the nuances present in more naturally occurring relationships.

The parties to which the boy accompanied the nightclub proprietor usually went on till dawn. At these libertarian gatherings the boy met many members of the bohemian demi-monde: musicians and budding actors, not to mention lots of females in search of a little craziness and out for a good time. It was a milieu where louche behaviour was commonplace. To the boy, the scenes of abandon that resulted had an irresistible appeal. The attraction got him into some odd situations.

On one occasion he was sleeping with a beautiful girl when her brother, who was evidently in love with his sister, came to join them in the bed, to the consternation of the sister and the boy. An argument followed, which culminated in the brother being thrown out of the bed. (Some years later, the girl concerned married a pop star.) Another time, one evening at a cocktail party, the boy met the novelist Robin Maugham. He was not someone he had ever heard of before, though he was familiar with the novels and stories of his uncle, Somerset Maugham. Robin was in a group with three other men who gave the impression of being army types of the officer class. They took an immediate shine to the boy and spent most of the evening talking to him, to the exclusion of all the other guests.

The boy was very flattered to find himself the centre of attention in this way. It even seemed that the members of Robin's entourage were vying with each other to engage him in conversation. When the party was over, they invited the boy to come on afterwards and have dinner with them at a restaurant. It was only courtesy to accept. Moreover, he felt it could do his future prospects no harm to enlarge his circle of acquaintances. Ideas emerge through contact with others, especially when they are drawn from many different social levels.

Throughout the dinner the conversation continued to be mainly focused on the boy. They wanted to know everything they could about him: his background, his education, above all his ambitions in life. The boy was not accustomed to being fêted in this way, holding court to a group of admirers who hung on his every word. The deluge of attention went completely to his head. As the evening wore on, he became more and more animated, spilling out all sorts of private thoughts and feelings. With the dinner over, it was time for everyone to return to their respective houses. Niceties were exchanged and they all dispersed.

Three days passed before Robin Maugham made contact again. This time he invited the boy to have dinner with him and his three friends at his home. The boy could see no reason to decline and accepted the invitation. Everybody in the group greeted him warmly, and this time were less reserved and treated him with less formality. Robin cooked the dinner himself. It was superb, with all the trappings of a gourmet feast. The finest claret was served, and although the boy was not a great drinker normally, he was somehow coerced into imbibing more than usual. It was only as the atmosphere of male fellowship reached a disconcerting level that it began to dawn on him that there was a different purpose behind the flattery and attentiveness. Suddenly his demeanour changed. He became very fidgety on his seat and sweated with anxiety. The affinity that he thought had been there between him and Robin and his three friends suddenly evaporated. He began to look for a gracious way out that would cause no offence to his host or the guests who had shown him such hospitality and kindness. Their motivation was a matter for them; perhaps it was something beyond their control. He was not prepared to be judgemental about Robin and his friends, though he suddenly saw clearly what they hoped for from him: to enlist him into their inner circle.

In those days, the practice of homosexual acts was against the law in Britain and homosexual life was very much undercover as a result. The police set traps for those who sought to solicit other men for sexual purposes and some illustrious figures in society had been brought to court and sentenced to prison, their reputations in tatters. The boy, because of his old-fashioned upbringing and his strong orientation towards women, could never have contemplated getting into a situation where his sexuality was compromised. The idea of having a physical relationship with a man was anathema to him. The highly charged surroundings in which he now found himself overwhelmed him completely. All he could do was feign a sudden attack of illness (though he knew they would not believe it for a moment), make his apologies and dart out of the house before things went any further. He fled into the street in a state of panic and struggled to control it as he turned the corner.

In his agitation he went on walking the streets for a while, reflecting deeply on the events of the past few days, and deciding, to his great relief, that he would be able to put it all down to experience. It was an area where he was still naïve. None of Robin's friends had looked the part. They showed no signs of effeminacy or any of the other qualities consistent with popular homosexual stereotypes. But then, the boy considered, there had been great and fierce warriors in history, emperors and towering philosophers, whose sexual preferences had not been evident from their outward appearance. The result of it all was to set him thinking about issues he had never before considered.

A few years later, when the boy went to see Joseph Losey's film of *The Servant*, based on a novel of the same title by Robin Maugham and starring Dirk Bogarde, he understood many things that had not been clear to him when he first encountered the sexual ambiguities of Robin Maugham's social circle. Looking back, he felt no regrets. On the contrary, he was thankful for the manner in which that brief episode had opened his eyes to mankind's infinite variety when it came to matters of sexuality. He realized he had overreacted at Robin's house on the night in question because he lacked understanding and because he was facing a situation he didn't know how to handle without making a complete fool of himself. He had panicked, and panic can be as bad in its effects as excessive drink. Both can make us act in a silly, irrational manner, abandoning our normal sense of proportion.

It puzzled him how Britain, which claimed to be a tolerant, liberal society, could have such oppressive and muddled laws restricting the behaviour of its homosexual citizens. The law seemed to be badly in need of reform; certainly it seemed to go against all principles of human rights. A person's sexual preferences were a matter for themselves alone, of no concern to others. As with religion and race, sexuality related profoundly to the individual, and any discrimination deserved to be outlawed.

The jazz club soon closed. It had been run on a very short lease. The boy was therefore out of a job again, but the proprietor, his former employer, would do one more thing to influence his life. The jazz band he led was being hired to play at a grand society wedding reception at London-derry House, a most exclusive venue in Park Lane; the proprietor invited the boy to come along with the band to enjoy the fun. It was a strange coincidence. The wedding was that of Quentin Crewe to his first wife, an American. (All his numerous subsequent marriages provided copy for most of the upper-class journals.) The boy had never met Quentin, but he was a very good friend of George Hutchinson, who had told him a lot about him. Like George, Quentin was a brilliant young journalist who worked for the formidable Lord Beaverbrook. He was also very well connected as a cousin of the former prime minister, Harold Macmillan. The whole affair was meticulously organized and the guest list was staggering – an eclectic mix of aristocrats, politicians, celebrities and representatives of the media.

The grand company danced the night away as the band swung to vigorous rhythm after vigorous rhythm in Dixie-land mode. The soloist for the vocal numbers was the well-known – and delectable – jazz singer Annie Ross, who enthralled the revellers with her rich, melodic voice. It thrilled the boy beyond measure to be part of English society's most glittering gathering that night in Mayfair, even if it was only for a brief interlude of a few hours; and then to have the good fortune to be sitting next to Annie Ross as a passing photographer (the word 'paparazzi' was not yet in vogue) snapped a picture. Later the boy was able to secure a print of the photograph and proudly give it a permanent place in his album.

As the reception ended, the boy and the band were invited to go on to Quentin's apartment in Dolphin Square for a celebratory breakfast. George Hutchinson was surprised to see the boy at the party; even more astonished to hear of the chain of circumstances that brought him there. Fate has the habit of playing odd games with people's lives. It was much later that the boy came face to face with Quentin in a different context and they forged a friendship that lasted till Quentin's death.

During his time at the jazz club, the boy had been a person of no fixed abode. Thanks to Miss Willmott, though, he never lacked a place where he could sleep. The house in Oakley Gardens was as yet an empty property, the sale of Miss Wilmott's lease having still not gone through in the wake of her move to Streatham. Miss Willmott therefore agreed that he could camp out temporarily in the basement. It was a spooky experience to live alone in the empty house formerly inhabited by so many people, and it brought back memories of his first encounters with England in late 1949. In the basement, he slept on a mattress on the floor. It reminded him of the time in Nazareth when he was living with his grandmother and great-aunt and had also slept on a mattress with a blanket, which was all the bedding they could afford. But this time he was surrounded by books, many of which he read. As he found it hard to sleep during the day after the excitements of his night life, his tactic was to take up a book and read it till sleep overtook him. The job as a bouncer turned his body-clock topsy-turvy and started to take its toll on his health. It was necessary for him to move on and follow up Adam's offer. Another phase of his life was about to begin in the house of Mrs Rudzka in Acton.

Mrs Rudzka was a remarkable woman. She was a Polish writer and historian whose speciality was the history of Poland in the eighteenth and nineteenth centuries. Among her writings was an important study of the Polish uprising against Russia in 1863. She had lived in Poland throughout the war, but escaped in 1947 after her country became part of the Soviet bloc. Her husband, Adam Rudzki, after whom the boy's friend Adam was named, was an economist who had been in the Polish army in 1939 and escaped to Sweden after the Nazis took over; he then arrived in Britain via France to join the Polish army in exile. At the time when the boy went to live in the house in Acton, Mr Rudzki had gone to take up residence in the United States with Adam's elder brother, Marek, and was already active there in promoting Polish freedom in the ideological fight against Communism. The plan was for Mrs Rudzka to join them in America once Adam had completed his engineering degree. Meanwhile she remained on her own in London.

Walentyna Rudzka herself came from a distinguished family of Polish intellectuals, the Nagorskis. One brother, Juljusz, was a well-known architect and artist who was shot by the Germans during the Warsaw uprising. Two other brothers, Zygmunt and Adam (known as Adal), were prominent lawyers. Zygmunt was active in the Polish government in exile during the war, and after the war

Adal represented companies seeking compensation from the Polish communist regime. Another brother, Bohdan, head of the Polish-American shipping line, was torpedoed in the Atlantic in the early 1940s and survived two weeks adrift in a lifeboat.

Apart from all these family connections and her own talents, Mrs Rudzka was a very liberal person who loved the company of young people. She had a great sense of humour and was tolerant of other people's foibles. Before he went to live in Acton the boy decided he must put his cards on the table. He did not want to conceal the fact that he was going through a wild phase in his life and would be wanting to bring girls back to his room. Mrs Rudzka took this in her stride and they made a pact that she would respect his private life, and he would be allowed to bring his women to the house, so long as his activities did not impinge on her own living arrangements. In the mornings, if she knew he had no female company, she liked to come to his room for a chat, so he got into the habit of slipping a note under her door, when he arrived back at night with a companion, to alert her that the room was out of bounds. It was an arrangement that Mrs Rudzka stuck to punctiliously.

One night he returned home with a French girl he had met at the coffee bar in Hanway Street. She was a tall, slender young woman with a stunning face and seductive body. He slipped the usual note under Mrs Rudzka's bedroom door and the pair proceeded to bed. They were already in the throes of passion and could hardly get their clothes off quickly enough, but the instant gratification he had anticipated was not forthcoming. The girl was not going to let him take her without making him sweat first. She certainly knew how to excite her man, but every time he was proudly raring to go, she crossed her legs in such a way as to obstruct further progress. In the meantime, she affected to caress a soft Turkoman rug given to the boy by his father, which he used as a blanket. Seeing how she liked the rug, the boy, in his desperate state of arousal, said it would be hers in the morning. The offer seemed to do the trick. She immediately became more receptive and, of her own accord, made matters easier. As she moved towards orgasm she began to grunt and groan, so that the boy had to press a hand over her mouth, mindful of not disturbing Mrs Rudzka's sleep and perhaps even waking her.

Afterwards, the couple fell into a peaceful slumber, until they were disturbed by a persistent knocking on the door. It was Mrs Rudzka in a state of agitated concern. She insisted that she must have a few words with the boy in private. He quickly covered himself and went out into the corridor. He should, she begged him, really reconsider. Was he going to sacrifice his treasured rug, a gift from his father, just for the sake of a moment of folly. The boy could hardly believe his ears as the implications started to dawn on him. The French girl had never had any intention of taking his rug; he had not expected that she would. It had only been part of a game of sexual barter to heighten the physical tension and ultimately arrive at an enhanced level of satisfaction. But the cat was out of the bag so far as Mrs Rudzka's secret was concerned.

It turned out that she awaited his return each night in a high state of eagerness. Whenever he had a girl with him, she listened avidly to everything that went on in his bedroom through the thin partition wall that separated her room from his. The solitary life she had been leading in Acton was suddenly transformed into one of anticipation and excitement. She never knew what might happen next, and it was seldom that the boy disappointed her. He could be relied upon to create the sort of night-time incidents that she found so diverting. The boy revelled in the added dimension of freedom this knowledge gave him. There was no doubting that, in a quaint sort of way, Mrs Rudzka relished her new-found role of observer – perhaps even of voyeur.

After the colourful experience of being a nightclub bouncer, the boy turned back to his original ambition and decided he ought to focus on looking for a job in journalism. He could wait no longer and knew he must make a genuine effort. He sought the help of his friend George Hutchinson, who arranged for him to become a member of the National Union of Journalists, so that he would be able to move straight into an appointment in the field if one became available. But by now it was late 1956, a time when jobs generally were hard to come by. His insistence on being a journalist narrowed his chances of finding work even further. He signed on at the Ministry of Labour and drew the dole for about eight months.

During his time of unemployment, books became more important to him than ever before. Literature, it seemed to him, opened windows on to life in its infinite variety. It provided a feast for the mind. Each book he read added to his stock of knowledge of the world. He explored the French tradition in its whole range, from Stendhal, Victor

Hugo, Molière and Racine to Colette, André Gide, Marcel Pagnol, Jean Anouilh, Jean Cocteau and André Malraux. Albert Camus settled next to Jean-Paul Sartre amid the procession of volumes, and from other parts of Europe came Stefan Zweig, Thomas Mann and Franz Kafka; from Russia there emerged the figure of Maxim Gorky. He was drawn to the Americans, too, with their imaginative vigour in exploring expressive new possibilities for the English language in their individual styles of writing. The novelists William Faulkner, Ernest Hemingway and John Steinbeck could excite the imagination and engage passion and sympathy for the most unlikely characters; as did the playwrights Eugene O'Neill, Arthur Miller and Tennessee Williams. It was a rich period in American consciousness that perhaps became rather underrated later on.

Although in whiling away his time in coffee houses and the constant pursuit of women the boy seemed to be wasting away his youth, he spent hours each day reflecting on what should be his aim in life. By his reckoning the current phase could not last. He saw it as a period during which indiscretions and excesses were to be tolerated so long as they were seen as valuable experiments in preparation for a more structured life later on. He knew this was not his chosen course and therefore accepted things as they came without having any worries about the future.

The boy also wrote a lot. The innate corruptness of human nature was his particular theme as he sought to analyse the morbid side of man's existence. He did not write with the idea of getting anything into print. The process was more to do with an exploration of the darker areas within his mind. In his social life he was completely the opposite: no introvert but an eternal optimist who was confident that he would reach his goal in the end, even if it was not yet clearly defined. The problem here was that he lacked the patience to bide his time for long. He wanted things to happen immediately, and if they failed to do that, he soon lost interest. He did not mind the pressure; time was his real adversary. He would have to learn to curb his obsession with getting results fast, which some believe is the devil's way to wreck things.

And what of boredom? It is similar to depression; it arrives like an intruder in the night to pounce when least expected. The boy was constitutionally prone to it. Variation itself generated the energy he channelled in many directions. It was necessary for him to be living on the edge, a state that kept him constantly exploring possibilities and pushing back boundaries. Meeting a challenge put him on a high most of the time: it was a key to what made him tick – his ultimate *raison d'être*.

During this period of enforced inactivity, conflicting thoughts were cluttering his mind. To live for today was the easy option. It relieved the immediate pressures. But not to have to think about tomorrow, however comforting, could have an anaesthetizing effect; it was also the ultimate in irresponsibility and did not suit his temperament. He was in a turmoil partly because he sensed that things could not stay the way they were. At least at Mrs Rudzka's house he had a solid base and some-one who was kind, hospitable and sympathetic. But all this, he knew, could come to an end. Where would he then find his refuge? Was it inevitable that he must leave the comforts of the house in Acton and return to the hard life he had sometimes had to endure before, living in cramped bed-sitters in semi-derelict buildings with no proper heating? Only time would tell.

Mrs Rudzka often reproached him for being a dreamer. She urged him to do something more constructive with his life. Talent, in her opinion, might well emerge in its own good time, but meanwhile it had to be helped on its way. It did not matter what sort of job he took. Picking and choosing had never necessarily earned anyone a living. She made these points frequently, but however forcefully she expressed them, the boy remained adamant. In his own mind, it was just that his time had not yet arrived, and when it did it would have been well worth waiting for. He and Mrs Rudzka had many lively disagreements on the issue, but the relationship never faltered and they remained the closest of friends.

An odd episode did occur at the time when Mrs Rudzka was putting pressure on the boy to find a job. One afternoon, as the boy was lounging in a coffee bar, having an animated conversation with a beautiful girl he had just met, a man intruded on them at their table. He was a film scout, he announced, who worked for a film agency in Soho. The agency was looking for a girl to fill a role, and here was a young lady who matched the specifications exactly. The agency was only a few yards along the street from the coffee bar; he could escort her there straight away.

The girl's immediate reaction was to be uninterested, but the boy saw it as an offer full of exciting potential. He needed to work hard to persuade her that this could be the sort of opportunity that comes along only once in a lifetime. To refuse to go would be a gratuitous act of self-denial. How would she ever know what a glowing future she might be turning down if she just walked away? Slowly she came round to the idea, and they agreed with the scout that she would go with him, provided the boy accompanied them. They set off for the agent's office, where the walls of the large room were lined with photographs of actors available for work. At the far end sat a woman of about fifty, heavily made up and with an oriental cast to her features. A colourful parrot sat in a large cage quite close to her desk.

The agent began to talk to the girl, but it was soon evident that she was unimpressed. The girl's stunning looks alone were not going to make her into film material, she pointed out. Lovely as she was to look at, she lacked the fire and charisma that are vital ingredients for those who make the grade in the film world. As the agent delivered her harsh judgement, she was interrupted in mid-flow as the parrot sprang in with the line, 'Shut up, you old cow!' which it then repeated again and again. The agent became extremely annoyed with the bird, and explained how all this was the fault of an idiotic woman assistant who had prattled gibberish non-stop. Finally, in despair, she had shouted at the woman, 'Shut up, you old cow!' The parrot, instantly imprinted, took up the phrase and kept coming out with it shamelessly whenever there were visitors in the office. In the boy's view, the parrot was the real star of the show. The bird was unforgettable. He had never found anything so funny. The more the imprecations of her owner fell about her head, the more she gyrated and preened on her perch as if immensely pleased with herself. The boy was almost in a state of collapse with laughter.

It was clear that the exercise of getting the girl into movies was futile, so he suggested to the agent that he would be available to work in the film industry, as an extra if necessary, so long as she thought there was a chance of this leading on to more important film parts in the future. The agent looked him up and down, rather impressed by his self-assurance. She took his assertion that, at the age of fifteen, he had had acting experience back home in Haifa with the pinch of salt it deserved. Then she suggested that he get a studio photograph taken of himself and bring it in to her that same afternoon. By next day, a photograph of the boy, with available artist stamped across it, was gracing the wall of the agent's office among those of all the other hopefuls. Many work opportunities did subsequently come about as a result, but none of them was significant, and every time it happened he was nowhere to be found. If he had not been busy elsewhere each time one of those calls came through, who knows what different directions his life might have taken?

There was never a dull moment in that extraordinary year in Acton. Mrs Rudzka wanted to participate in any fun that was going, especially when the boy brought home a crowd of young people, mostly female. The boy had gone into a phase where he enjoyed smoking cannabis through a narghile he had brought with him from Nazareth. Having heated pieces of medical charcoal on a gas stove till they were red-hot, he would sit on the floor among his visitors and place the glowing embers in the allotted place in the narghile. The cannabis had been mixed with tobacco to give it extra burning power, and as the group took turns to draw the smoke into their lungs and test its effects, a heavenly smell ascended and crept through the house. Inevitably Mrs Rudzka would arrive to find the source of the smell and insist on joining the circle. Reluctantly they allowed her to sit and smoke with them – a blank refusal would have been an obvious give-away – but none of them dared tell her she was smoking hashish. The boy watched anxiously every time she inhaled what she had been told was an aromatic herbal concoction, since he knew she had a heart-murmur and feared that by taking part she might be tempting fate.

The *entente* the boy and Mrs Rudzka had arrived at over his sexual habits did not always save him from embarrassment. Sex can be bliss or torment. Practised in moderation and at the right time, it can be the most delightful pleasure a human being can imagine; taken to extremes, it can become an all-consuming and perilous navigation of the outer edges of experience. Out of control, it can inflict bodily as well as mental anguish – a result perhaps as destructive as enforced celibacy can be.

One night the boy returned home with a very striking blonde he had met at the usual coffee bar near Tottenham Court Road. Mrs Rudzka must have been already asleep when they arrived back, but she woke up as they were negotiating the stairs and came out on to the landing in her dressing-gown to bid the young couple good-night. Her doing this made the boy particularly conscious of the thin wall between the rooms, and how Mrs Rudzka would hardly need to strain her ears, in the silence of the night, to hear the lovers' conversation.

As soon as the boy was in bed with the blonde, the inevitable sex play started. At first things went at a reasonably modest tempo, but suddenly the girl seemed caught up in a rising crescendo of such intensity and power that she could no longer control the level of her sighs and groans. It was a mad display of raw lust that took the boy by surprise. Her body began to twist, as if she were dancing to a jive band. The bed shook alarmingly and seemed close to the point of collapse. Things had gone beyond the boy's control. He found himself on the receiving end of someone else's desires; he had to settle for a passive role and try his utmost to stop the situation deteriorating into something that was going to destroy Mrs Rudzka's equanimity totally. He had no doubt that she would be listening to all these goings-on. All he could do was attempt a kind of damage limitation by letting the blonde's frenzy carry her to a satisfactory conclusion.

It was wishful thinking. She continued from peak to peak of climax without ever reaching an ultimate summit. The intensity grew and grew; there was no sign of any end to it. For every orgasm she reached, there was another to follow in its wake. There were no pauses in between, no moments for rest. At a loss to know what to do, the boy jumped out of bed in a state of panic. He headed for the bathroom, which lay across the landing, directly opposite Mrs Rudzka's door, and locked himself in. After about ten minutes, the blonde came looking for him. He refused to open the bathroom door, but urged her to go back to bed, saying he would join her there shortly.

Before Mrs Rudzka had time to come out of her room to find out what was happening, the blonde had fled back to the boy's bedroom. The boy meanwhile settled down to spend the rest of the night in the bathtub and silence filled the house. Remaining sleepless for a while, he thought of his time in Venice with the Argentinian doctor. There was a superficial similarity. In both cases pleasure turned into delirium. He was reminded of the agony and ecstasy which had consumed him during that remarkable formative encounter. Yet there were differences. The earlier episode had involved his becoming familiar with a woman's body and all its hidden secrets; his initiation into the mysteries of the vagina, where life really had its source. The second episode was an exercise in pure lust, which had misfired. It was as simple as that.

When he woke in the morning, after about four hours of troubled sleep in the bath, he was aching all over. He accepted that there had had to be a price to pay. Returning to the fray with the blonde had been out of the question. She was a nice girl in every respect, except that she became truly lethal when sexually aroused: a tornado in bed that few men could have handled. Even in her old age, Mrs Rudzka looked back on her memories of these incidents and disturbances with nostalgia. The truth was that she was inwardly rather bemused at the lengths to which a male of the human species was prepared to go to achieve sexual gratification.

The atmosphere became a little less electrically charged when her son Adam came home from his university course at the end of each week. Adam had recently overhauled his Alvis car, and driving out to look for some attractive female talent to meet up with and bring home became a favourite weekend recreation. Having a car of such a prestigious type seemed to make the operation easier. Most of the girls they met liked the idea of being driven rather than having to go anywhere by public transport: the attitude seemed to be that if they were going to sin they might as well do it in style. Mostly the car's attraction worked. There were, however, occasions when the whole adventure ended on a sour note. When this happened it was invariably the boy's fault. The problem arose when he had been canoodling with one particular girl for part of the evening and then, without warning, turned his attention to one of her friends and tried to start on the same exercise again from the beginning. The consequence was that both the girls concerned would get into a huff and insist on being driven home.

Adam was the only one who could drive, so he would have to curtail his own plans for the evening and irritably convey the boy's failures to wherever they wished to be taken. Any progress that Adam had been making with his own potential companion of the night collapsed in ruins. It was happening all too often for Adam's liking. He came to feel that he was being used and was determined to regain control of the situation and put an end to these disruptions. He started to put pressure on the boy to give an undertaking that he would, in future, stick to the one girl and refrain from trying to seduce her friends at the same time. It was an unhealthy situation that led only to embarrassment and unpleasantness. When that agreement failed to hold, Adam conjured up the idea of the boy learning to drive. This would minimize the risk of his having to drive irate girls home in the middle of the night through no fault of his own. He would himself teach the boy to drive. That would take care of the problem. Once he had passed his driving test, the boy would then be able to drive his own girls home, without spoiling anyone else's fun.

The boy was happy to learn and the lessons began without delay. He was soon making appreciable progress, but the dangers of over-confidence lay in wait for him as they do for everyone. One day he offered to drive Mrs Rudzka and Adam from Acton up to the West End. Mrs Rudzka, being a great sport and wanting to do all she could to encourage the boy, applauded the idea and overruled Adam's protestations that it was utter recklessness to be attempting such a journey prematurely. They set off, with Mrs Rudzka sitting happily and comfortably in the back and Adam in the passenger seat in a state of foreboding.

Everything went smoothly till they came to Shepherd's Bush Green and Adam protested to the boy that he was going too fast and travelling much too close to a trolleybus in front. Instead of putting his foot on the brake to slow the car, the boy panicked and pressed down on the accelerator instead. One of the front wheels of the Alvis ran up on to the trolleybus platform and two passengers waiting to alight had to beat a rapid retreat into the interior to avoid injury. Meanwhile Adam had grabbed the steering wheel and the car and the trolleybus juddered to a sudden halt, still locked in their unwelcome embrace. Mrs Rudzka disappeared from view as the jolt of the impact slumped her down on to the seat. Luckily she was unhurt, and no one else suffered any injuries. The incident, however, helped to explain why the boy never had another driving lesson, and never again, in all his life, felt the ambition to drive.

Even as a child of eleven, the boy was captivated by the written word; prose, poetry, even the art of calligraphy – all held an endless fascination for him. Because of his frail health, he rarely engaged in sport; or, to be more precise, he was never allowed to do so. The time that he had on his hands as a result was mostly spent on reading and writing, or on analysing political events in the manner of a grown-up. He was unduly sophisticated for his years and preferred the conversation of adults (which added substantially to his store of knowledge) to the company of children his own age. He already saw his future as lying elsewhere from his family environment in Haifa. He did not know where that would be, but the world he built around himself out of his vivid imagination was that of a dreamer. This world had no conventional boundaries and little regard for the established rules that had so far governed, perhaps orchestrated, his life.

He was a revolutionary at heart, in spite of possessing a pronounced sensitivity – a trait not generally associated with those who seek to enforce radical change or foment rebellion. He loved to read the works of those philosophers with whom he felt he had common ground. He could not hope to grasp everything he read, but the challenge of trying to unlock the complexities of their arguments exercised his intellect, nourishing the mind in the way that food nourished the body. The boy was constantly scribbling things down; no matter where he happened to be he was quick to observe anything bizarre or out of the ordinary so he could record it for future reference. He had a love of learning that grew with him into his adult years and remained with him through all that happened in his life.

The boy's habit of writing to try to give voice to his imagination became a refuge for him when he first arrived in England. Alone in his room at Miss Wilmott's, he battled with how he could stretch the possibilities of the English language in his creative writing. He wrote a piece he called 'Between Night and Morning', using a – no doubt outmoded – parable style for a prose poem. It began in tones of melancholy:

> Hush my heart, the sky does not hear you.
> Hush, the ether is burdened with lamentations,
>   and wailings will not carry your songs and chants.
> Hush, the phantoms of the night do not care for
>   the whispers of your secrets, and the processions
>   of darkness do not stop before your dreams.

As the poem proceeded, he imagined his thoughts in the form of a boat:

> Hush my heart and hear me speaking.
> My thought was yesterday a ship on the undulating
>   waves of the sea and voyaging with the air from
>   shore to shore.
> The ship of my thought was empty save for seven
>   glasses full of various colours resembling the
>   colours of the rainbow in bloom.
> And there came a time when I grew weary of
>   wandering on the surface of the sea and said,
>   'I shall return with the empty ship of my soul
>   to the port of my native country.'
> I painted the corners of my ship with yellow colours
>   for the sunset, green for the heart of spring, blue

for the linen of the sky, red for fraternal love, and sketched on its sail and rudder strange pictures which attracted the eyes and brightened the view.

When the ship arrives, the people come out to welcome it with drums and trumpets, but all they see is the painted exterior. The ship inside is empty. It sails away again and gathers treasures from the seas of the world, but now when it returns with its hold full of earth's wonders, the people only regard it with derision. All they can see is the outward appearance of things.

When he was in Stafford, the boy's spare time was very limited. He did as much overtime as he could in the English Electric factory to earn extra money. The living conditions in the homes where he stayed were hardly conducive to creative effort and the whole atmosphere was rather stifling. It was a depressing time for him. He considered that his social roots had been put down in London and he was not happy with having to live any-where else. He knew he must somehow counteract the dangers of sinking into a clinical depression. One pre-scription he arrived at was to embark on writing letters to all his friends to give him solace. Any time he had over from that activity he allocated to composing short pieces of prose on the imaginary encounters of opposites. He was coming more and more to see the world in terms of contrasts: the beautiful as opposed to the ugly, evil in conflict with goodness, light breaking through the darkness and life walking hand in hand with death. Each extreme had its own role and special significance, but the extremes were at the same time interdependent. No extreme could exist without its opposite: the train of thought was an absorbing one.

A piece he wrote in Stafford was called 'Conflict between Opposites'. In his imagination he saw a gigantic, grotesque figure raise itself up on the summit of a mountain in the moonlight to address the moon with special pleading.

> O Queen of the Heavens . . . I have travelled many weary miles for this audience, I have climbed precipitous and hostile rocks. I have braved heat and cold, that the winds may carry my voice to your gracious ear, bearing the burden of my one small request.
>
> As your light reveals, I am indeed ugly. Through long ages have I suffered because my appearance causes men to shudder. It is such that I cannot bear to see my own reflection mirrored in a pool of still water.
>
> Therefore, O Queen, I pray you, make me good to look upon. Make me handsome and fair of face.

The Moon replies:

> O Son of the Unfaithful, you come with a wish that has been denied because of your evil heart. You have transformed beauty into ugliness, you have wrecked loveliness, you have destroyed fairness of form and face. It is not a change of face and figure that you need, but a change of soul. You cannot borrow beauty as I borrow it from the Sun.

The Figure presses on with his request:

O Queen of the Heavens, I am the most obedient of
all your slaves. You can give me beauty as you
give all things on earth beauty. You give your
pale, soft light to mills and alleyways, to crude and
clumsy things. And lo, your magic touch makes
them as lovely as lilies.

Give me, I beseech you, beauty also. I am most
wise. My wit is subtle, and none can match me in
persuasiveness. Sages and philosophers stammer or
fall silent when met by my matchless arguments.
None is so clever as to delude me, none so
cunning as to outwit me.

The Moon acknowledges that all that he says is true but
asks to what purpose he has put his great gifts:

You have used them to snare the innocent, to
destroy the wise, to bring derision upon the
ignorant. You have employed flattery to trip the
weak and vain, and you have used terror to bring
down the strong.

She does not accept that he can learn humility, or that
beauty of face could give him humility. When the Figure
promises that he will charm poets, painters and architects if
freed from his ugliness, and build vast and stately cities, she
does not doubt it, but has no wish to see such cities:

They are merely gigantic traps in which millions of
men are caught. It is in cities that your darkest
deeds have been done. It is in cities that all the
seeds you plant ripen. Lying, cheating, killing are

three of these things . . . You seem to forget that I
have looked down upon all the cities that man has
ever raised. I saw Sodom, Babylon, Nineveh and
Tyre. I saw Thebes, Athens, Pompei and Rome.
Some of those cities were jewels, shining with so
many splendours that they dazzled the eyes of
men. Yet the people in them were corrupt, cruel,
lascivious and full of guile.

Finally the Figure concedes:

It seems, O Queen, that I am to remain ugly.

And the Moon replies that she cannot give him beauty:

That must come from within yourself . . . Only
when your thoughts are pure, when your heart is
full of good intentions, when your soul is inspired
by truth and goodness and beauty, only then can
you have eternal beauty. Therefore begone, for I
cannot bear to look upon you longer.

The Figure vanishes, and there follows a universal silence,
broken only by the long and wistful sighs of the wind.

The boy was intrigued by the power complementary
opposites exert over our lives. This happens regardless of
the far-reaching impact they also have on our intellectual
evolution with the onset of maturity. He began to see
that there was also a parasitic dimension as these factors fed
on the mind. This, too, was largely overlooked, because
superficiality remained the easiest way to define the
indefinable. Few dared to delve deeply into the origin of
those causes that they saw as the reasons behind their very

existence, for each had an advantage in denying alternative versions of the truth.

Beauty inspired music, poetry – artistic creativity in all its sublime forms. Evil brought conflict, desecrated noble values, ravished innocence and fuelled temptation at its most base. The irony was that evil in the end gave birth to goodness, for extremity could bring in its wake extraordinary reversals. As in nature, the storms of conflict blew themselves out and gave way to repose and tranquillity. Light nurtured and boosted growth in nature, while darkness induced rest. Each element was equally necessary to maintain the ecological balance.

Death, as the conclusion of life, hovered inexorably, reminding mortals of the transitory nature of terrestrial existence. Yet death could be a welcome relief, even a friend, when all else had failed. Certain fanatics even celebrated death as the ultimate sacrifice, which they believed would unlock the doors of heaven. The civilized and the barbaric alike had a special relationship with death. Religious devotees saw it as the final moment of redemption before eternal life. Yet in the end all these mysteries of polarity were too complex to unravel. The boy would pour his thoughts out on paper, in the hope that elements might emerge to illuminate more clearly the uncertainties that he had racing through his mind.

While in Stafford he also tried his hand at writing short stories. These featured the same boldness of ideas, but were in search of the shape and style they needed to put them across. One, called 'The Dance Hall Girl', described the scene in the sort of city dance hall that was still the focus for the social life of young people in the 1950s. It picked up on the changes in dance convention that were then in the air:

> On the one side, the orthodox dancers swayed with the music, following the conventional, less exhausting steps. On the other were dancers who indulged any and every step, many of them ugly, clumsy improvisations which were merely confusing and bereft of all rhythm. A couple in the far corner of the hall were performing an extremely strenuous dance, their own version of a barbarian love sequence. The subtle gestures and the supple movements of their bodies at times revealed sex in its most acute form, thrilling the young people who knotted about them.

In contrast with this, there was a genuine performer, a solitary black man from Africa:

> He was doing it all after the manner of his own people, with agility, grace and a remarkable sense of artistic inspiration. It was a skilful display of an art which the new world has borrowed, without acknowledgement, from the old. In it there was nothing new, for the passion typified was as old as man and equally enduring. The black man, though exhausted, kept on dancing, whipped on by the music, oblivious of the outside world, defying the prejudice and unkindness in the hearts of men.
>
> Close by, meanwhile, a crowd of bebop boys was jiving in the modern American manner, but they lacked that depth of feeling which makes dancing an unconscious art. They were not absorbed by the music.

Instead they were its slaves, spending their energies in a futile effort to match their movements to its rhythm.

The scene then became phantasmagoric, leading up to the narrator finding himself dancing with a Salome-like figure:

Here was the spirit of youth in all its boundless aspects; in its indomitable search for erotic adventure, the escapades, the follies, the whims, the intoxication of the nerves . . . The dancers , with pale, sick faces, strained features, half-doped eyes, whirled, swung and clenched to the frenetic music of the band . . . I was overcome with a compelling desire to take part in this eruption of gaiety and found myself jiving with the devil's own image of temptation . . . Her lips burned with the fire of cupidity and in her eyes was a light never seen on earth.

The couple danced themselves to a standstill. As he leant over her collapsed figure, she opened her eyes and he saw the promise of a night of love such as few had ever known.

While this story was, in its immature way, about the combination of the sacred and profane in ecstasy, another, called 'The Last Noble Breath', attempted to deal with the whole problem of love and loss. Here the narrator faced the imminent death of his partner after a life of complete understanding and sharing – the perfect union that everyone longs for but few attain. 'I am the one who should be dying,' he protests. 'That would be easier.'

'Yes, it is hard to live at times,' she said, 'harder than it is to die. But life is more than a bond of affection which unites two people. It is much more than the love of a man for a woman. Life is achievement, the answer to a challenge, the realization of hopes and ambitions. Your purpose is not yet complete . . . Only when you have created the beauty and uttered the truth will you be ready to rejoin me . . . The universe is grounded on beauty and based on truth.'

'Is it?' he asked, and only by a great effort did he restrain himself from crying out. 'What beauty is there in you dying, what goodness? . . . '

'A rose is very beautiful, my darling, but it lingers a very short time. A few dancing days in the sun while it flashes splendour from golden brightness, and then it withers and begins to perish. So much beauty for such a short time. But that is not surprising, really. The creator has such an immense store of beauty . . . and you know, too, that all his worlds are wonderful . . . Look at the sky. It has more worlds than men can ever number, all bright and all lending brightness to each other. They fade, but others take their place, and the world and all infinity is charged with a beauty that is renewed and increased.'

'But such a large universe,' he said, 'such a large universe in which to be alone.'

'You will never be alone,' she said, so softly that he could barely hear her . . . 'Be proud and happy for me . . . And I shall be waiting for you.'

These prose writings from Stafford were perhaps not so much stories as imagined situations reflecting the boy's inner preoccupations as he came to terms with the world about him. After he returned to London, his time in Acton at Mrs Rudzka's house was not only a period when his wildest physical impulses were gratified. It was also a productive period in a different sense. Although on the one hand he had constructed a hedonistic environment about himself, on the other he went on trying to express his inner thoughts in a morbid sort of writing that had a poetic edge to it. His dream since childhood had been to write, for in writing it is possible to give free rein to one's most intimate feelings without constraint; writing is a solitary, painful task but it may dare to show its faceless side without fear of a more tangible confrontation. His literary creativity was perhaps at its zenith during those days when he felt most forlorn and isolated. At those times he was acutely aware of being almost an orphan. He thought of how his family had been brutally separated by the events that led to the formation of the state of Israel. One way or another, they had all ended up living in what was a foreign land, for the Palestine he knew and loved had ceased to exist except as an idea in the heart. Although the family ties remained as strong as ever, he was having to fend for himself in a situation where it would have been unthinkable to ask for any assistance, especially on the financial front. Dreams help to maintain morale, but they can be very dangerous if they lull us into a false sense of reality. The rich can implement their dreams almost at will, but those less fortunate have to tread a rocky road. For them dreams can only be made to come to true through toil and sweat and a steely resolve.

One piece in the sequence of his writings in Acton, 'A Pause among the Graves', was typical in its gothic, over-the-top, possibly hasish-induced imagery:

I thrust at the gate of the dead and walked in the lair
of ghosts with lurid face and broken heart. I
entered the placid cemetery where the bitter
secrets of many poor souls flapped as leaves in the
wind. The phantoms of life, like the nocturnal
beasts, quit their dens in the darkness of night.
They terrified men of feeble heart and abducted
their will to a hell of dumbness. These creatures
are the slaves of humanity – the slaves of their
passion and enjoyments. I stepped along the
clumsy, sinuous paths and stumbled on the skulls
and bones of the wretched people who had died
under a veil of pain, love and patriotism . . .
I sat in the place of rendezvous where I could mourn
my beloved and kiss the earth she dwelt in.
I sat and heard the floating whispers of the soft
breeze swaying with the flowers mutant with
reverence and awe . . .
There I bent over the grave of my spirit and watered
the lilies, the symbol of her soul, with a flood of
tears – tears of the fragrant blood of the victims of
love.

There was much else in the same vein: a morose sort of
writing, but the words were signposts on the road to
maturity, however obscure the goal remained. In Acton,
while he sat for many hours reading and writing, he also
pondered philosophically. Were we predestined to follow
a given path? Or could we truly be masters of our own
destinies irrespective of time and place? He asked the
questions repeatedly. Was a person cast into the wilder-

ness ever likely to achieve the same measure of success as someone born into a thriving society that offered opportunities every step of the way? What would have become of him if he had remained in Nazareth? Could he have lived happily near to nature and survived the vicissitudes of everyday life as his grandmother and great-aunt had done in the past? Times had changed, he argued. Their sort of spartan existence – pitted against the elements, winning nature's benefits only through constant struggle – was no longer regarded with the same degree of respect and admiration.

At least the boy's tendency to dwell on these things sharpened his awareness and made his mind more analytical. All the time he was adding depth to his perceptions of beauty and ugliness, which to him represented the poles of good and evil. Their contrasting differences were another dimension that he needed to dissect if he was ever to understand the true meaning of life.

The morbidity in his writing sprang from the noticeable change in his lifestyle that came with his move to Acton. He was perceiving things through the perspective of jazz music intermingled with the occult. It was a weird period in his life when he was lost between distorted imagery and the real world. The one thing he knew was that nothing was for ever. The world's conventional forces must eventually compel him to turn back towards conformity. How this would happen he could not foresee. Meanwhile Mrs Rudzka provided an anchor point as Miss Willmott had done at an earlier stage of his time in England. Both these women had listened to him and accepted him as he was.

Outside his life in Acton, the boy kept up his contacts with all the friends he had made; he continued to be a regular visitor at the Garnetts in Maida Vale. Papp Garnett was as active as ever, never lacking an excuse to talk about his days in Palestine. The boy was amazed to discover what a small world it was. In Haifa, the Garnett home had been in Vine Street, only a stone's throw from Mountain Road, the location of the boy's family home. It had also been close by the Convent Dames de Nazareth, where the boy attended school with his sisters when he was very young. Papp first went to Palestine after the First World War to take up a post with the Colonial Service. He had risen to become the northern divisional engineer for the Palestine Post & Telegraph Company. His staff were so pleased with his even-handed treatment of both factions in those times of sporadic strife between the Arab and Jewish communities that they provided him with a document of safe passage. It was written in both Arabic and Hebrew to safeguard him should he fall into the hands of insurgents from either side during his widespread travels in the country. After his retirement in 1945 and his return to England, he was awarded the OBE.

Papp's anecdotes invariably held a special fascination. A favourite story concerned one of the guests at a cocktail party at the family house in Vine Street – a certain Mr Chester, who had recently been fitted out with a fine new set of dentures by the local dentist. Mr Chester happened to be leaning over the balcony of the veranda listening as Papp regaled the company with yet another humorous incident. At the denouement everyone roared with laughter, and Mr Chester laughed so hard that his false teeth flew out of his mouth and disappeared into the shrubbery below. After the group had recovered from this further piece of amusement, a search was mounted for Mr Chester's teeth among the plants and shrubs, but all in vain. They were finally found by the gardener next morning.

The story was one of many in similar vein that made Papp Garnett a raconteur *par excellence* and a most affable and entertaining host. Yet it seemed odd that Papp never talked about his first family, from before the time of his marriage to Afifi. It was as if there was a section of his life that could never be part of the life he had made with his new family. There seemed to be a contradiction in his character. His image of perfect family man was somehow called into question by the fact that, on the death of his wife, he had handed over the new-born baby, Nadia, for adoption by a childless couple. Could this have been a gesture of extreme generosity to give solace to a couple who could have no children of their own? Or was there something more complex, a darker shadow of rejection behind it? It would have been no burden for him to have kept and raised the baby since he had the means to do so. The mystery was to remain eternally unsolved. Rita, his eldest daughter from his first marriage, searched for her adopted sister, Nadia, and finally found her when they were both in their old age. Nadia was happy and contented. Whatever had happened had turned out well for her and the story ended reassuringly; the hint of there being some blemish or other over Papp Garnett's life was lifted.

Julie Garnett had meanwhile grown up into an attractive young woman, and had lost none of her tomboyish cheekiness. She combined Eastern beauty with Western panache. The special air she had about her always made the boy feel relaxed in her company. He could not fail to be aware of how she radiated an enchanting warmth. She possessed an enviable knack of fitting comfortably into any social environment. Julie's relationship with the boy was something special. It was based on the purest form of friendship and he considered her more in terms of family than anything else. Yet there was also perhaps some kind of sexual tension lurking deep within his subconscious, though it remained buried during all the time he knew her when they were young. The fact was that his heart raced whenever he was in her company, that she made him feel alive and at ease, and that he missed her if she was not around. If those were indications of love, then he must have loved Julie more than he was willing to admit at the time.

Some years later, Afifi told a close friend that Papp Garnett would never have consented to marriage between Julie and the boy. It was the old colonial attitude, she said. You can mix with the locals socially as a gesture of good will, but you don't intermarry with them; that would be unacceptable. It seemed to throw another odd contradictory light on Papp true nature. He was very fond of the boy and had treated him as a member of the family. It therefore seemed inconceivable that such snobbish prejudices could survive, lurking behind his bluff façade. Yet these attitudes were inherent in that generation of colonial civil servants. There was obviously a sharp irony in the fact that Papp Garnett had married Afifi, a Lebanese Arab, yet had been strongly opposed to the marriage of his daughter Grace to a Palestinian Arab. It was impossible to avoid feeling that there was a flaw somewhere in the character of this man whose integrity seemed unimpeachable.

When the boy was given two complimentary tickets by George Hutchinson for an important film première at the Odeon cinema in Leicester Square, he asked Julie to go with him. George had stressed that this was going to be a glamorous event and one should dress accordingly. Julie had no problem dolling herself up for the occasion and the boy managed to make himself look smart as well. Because of his poor financial situation, however, they had to devise special tactics to get there. It would have been far too expensive to take a cab all the way from Maida Vale, so they caught a No. 6 bus to Oxford Circus where they hailed a taxi to convey them the short remaining distance to Leicester Square. In this way they arrived in style. Improvisation was something the boy resorted to almost every day of the week. The glittering evening was a great success and gave the boy a taste of the sort of lifestyle he would soon be aspiring to.

Angelina, the girl he left behind in Stafford, stayed in touch. She had never given up hope that one day she might catch up with the boy in London. He was still clear in his mind, however, that it was a doomed relationship and from the start had been bound to fail. With the passage of time, the inevitable happened: the ties loosened and they drifted farther apart, each of them seeking new directions in life. He could never forget his 'Doris Day' singing girl, however, and the way she had enlivened his days and nights in a small provincial town when he was lonely at heart and in need of the sort of boost she was able to give so generously.

Mrs Rudzka continued to badger the boy about the need for him to find himself a job, any job. She genuinely feared for his future. If he did not find a job soon, he would just get used to idleness and it would be hard for him to shake off the habit. She was certain of it. On top of that, there was the dissolute sort of existence he insisted on leading, with the constant round of new young women crowding out the hope of anything resembling permanency or commitment. If promiscuity had never been a feature in his life before, why did it have to become one now? Again and again she warned him against his perverse way of looking at things. He would be better off finding himself a stable, steady girlfriend than bringing a new girl home almost every night of the week. She said all this with her usual graceful manner without upsetting the boy.

The advice was unconsciously heeded when he was introduced to a distant relation of Mrs Rudzka's and felt romantically drawn to the girl. Mrs Rudzka all at once grew quite perturbed and began to fear a scandal should the boy seduce her: according to reliable sources, the girl was still a virgin at the age of nineteen. At this point Adam Rudzki intervened as the boy's best friend and secured a promise from him that, come what may, he would not deflower his innocent relative. The consequence of this was that the boy and the girl started to engage in the sort of sexual activities that stopped short of deflowerment. The girl, for her part, became indignant that a pact had been agreed without her knowledge. She was intent on being seduced, and the *femme fatale* image that she tried to project suffered a dent as a result of this prohibition. Unsurprisingly, the relationship came to a dismal end before very long. The boy was upset at first, though he soon realized it had been a case of pure infatuation on both sides and the outcome was the only sensible one in the circumstances.

Then there was the fateful weekend when Adam brought home four young people for a drink. One of the men the boy already knew. One of the women was a Polish girl called Maria, who was there with a boy called Jack. The other girl, Maureen, had come with Maria. The boy was immediately attracted to Maureen and lost no time in getting into flirtatious mode with her. When the visitors left at the end of evening, he asked her for a date. She accepted without much fuss. Maureen was an extremely entertaining personality and had a kind and generous streak, but she also had some psychological peculiarities that only emerged as you got to know her. When she turned up on their first date she had Maria in tow, presumably because she was too nervous to come on her own. Either she needed Maria for reassurance or she thought there was safety in numbers. Whatever the reason, the evening went well. As soon as the girls heard that the boy was a table-tennis champion, they took him along to their office club – for they were also colleagues at work – to play table tennis with him. The boy partnered Maria for a game of doubles, and Maureen roped in another friend. Needless to say, the partnership between the boy and Maria won hands down. For the next date, both girls came to Acton to visit him at the house.

As the three of them sat in the living-room, the boy suddenly began to notice Maria in a new light. Seeking an excuse to be alone with her, even for just a few minutes, he suggested they go out on a short bus ride to bring back some drink while Maureen got on with preparing something to eat. Maria insisted that Maureen should be the one to go, but she changed her mind when Maureen encouraged her. On the way to the bus stop the boy tried to hold Maria's hand, but she pointedly made sure it stayed out of his reach. When he asked her if she would go on a date with him, she was taken aback with shock.

'Maureen is my best friend and you are supposed to be her boyfriend,' she protested. 'How can I possibly agree to a date with you?'

Back at the house Maria lost no time in telling her friend what had happened, but Maureen was surprisingly sanguine about the whole thing.

'Why not?' she asked Maria calmly.

It was the beginning of a new dawn in the boy's life. He fell in love with Maria, who was eighteen at the time. They embarked on a courtship and began to find out about each other's lives and to meet new friends. Maria was an only child, whose parents had like many others been separated by the war after Germany invaded Poland. Her mother had been forced into slave labour in Germany until the autumn of 1943, when she was transferred to a concentration camp. Throughout this time of crisis Maria was looked after, first, by a middle-aged German couple, and then, when the Allied bombing of Germany intensified, in the foster care of a family who had one teenage daughter. The daughter made herself spiteful to Maria by her constant bullying, in contrast with the mother of the family, who was kind and sheltered her as much as she could.

As the Russian army began its rapid march into Germany along the eastern borders and consolidated its territorial gains, there was chaos in the camp where Maria's mother was interned. She managed to escape in the confusion and, after an arduous search, was reunited with her daughter. They made their way to Italy and from there came on to England, where they settled in Shropshire with Maria's stepfather. Maria was then able to attend a school in Chester. When the boy first met her, she had been living in London for no more than four months.

There were now two major factors in the boy's life that promised to gladden Mrs Rudzka's heart. The first was that he was in steady courtship with a Polish girl. The second was that word had come from the Ministry of Labour warning him that his dole money would be stopped unless he accepted a job he had been offered in the City of London, with a French bank called Crédit Foncier d'Algérie et Tunisie. The boy had gone to the interview at the bank determined to create a bad impression to ensure he would fail it and be rejected as a candidate. After he arrived for his appointment with the manager, he had been totally negative about everything in every way he could think of. When asked whether he might like working in a bank, he retorted that he didn't know a debit from a credit. He'd be hopeless as a bank clerk, he said; his heart could never be in it. To his consternation, the manager seemed delighted with his responses. In the manager's view, someone coming into the business without any preconceptions was likely to make a better employee than someone who thought they knew it all. He therefore announced that he would inform the Ministry of Labour accordingly. Thus did the boy find himself facing the prospect of a career at last, though it was not one he wanted or had ever dreamed of seeking.

During this time, Mrs Rudzka and Adam had been getting on with their plans to move to New York to be reunited with the other half of their family. Adam was busy making arrangements to let the house in Acton so they could decide whether or not to sell it some time in the future. It meant the boy was going to have to find some alternative accommodation for the moment, and it so happened that his old room in Geraldine Road remained unoccupied. The uncle was now living in Birmingham, where he had taken up a job with the General Electric Company. He had decided not to sell the house in Wandsworth yet; he wanted to feel he was settled in his new job on a permanent basis first. It was therefore a convenient arrangement for the boy to move back to Geraldine Road, knowing it could only be temporary.

It still hit him hard, however, to be leaving the comforts of the house in Acton and starting to slum it yet again in a cold, lodging-house environment, bereft of any real warmth or an ambiance that suited him. He knew he had been utterly spoilt at Mrs Rudzka's and the move back to Geraldine Road must inevitably be a drastic change. His one comfort was that he had discovered a soulmate in Maria and they seemed to be gelling beautifully without even trying. Their relationship developed very quickly and in no time they had become inseparable companions. For both of them, it was a bonding like no other; it gave them the basis on which to start building their life together, long before they had a chance to think about the future.

Meanwhile, living in Geraldine Road was something that had to be endured. There had been no improvements made: the one bathroom and lavatory still served all the tenants in the house for their natural needs and functions. It was a nightmarish scenario that freaked the boy out on a daily basis – a situation he found almost impossible to cope with. Not having been a boy scout or conscripted into the army, he had never been forced into the situation of having to rough it with a crowd of other miscellaneous human beings. In that respect, he had been extremely sheltered. Such things weighed heavily on his mind – which nearly became unhinged every time he had to wait to use the bathroom. In a case of emergency, when nature could not possibly wait, he still had to strive to keep things under control. It left him with such a devastating legacy of paranoia about bathrooms and lavatories that he was reluctant ever afterwards to share facilities with anyone else.

His memory of the many months spent living in Mrs Rudzka's house helped to get him through this difficult spell. The times he had valued most in Acton were the dark winter nights when the weather was bad. Then he and Mrs Rudzka would sit by the fire to eat their evening meal together and converse well into the late hours. She was a revered figure in the Polish community as a historian of note. She had a deep and interesting intellect and was distinguished in everything she did. But the most endearing aspect of her character was her ability to understand the frailties of her fellow human beings and reserve moral judgement. She treated everyone with unfailing courtesy and charmed all those she met.

Mrs Rudzka had profound religious feelings, but they were not of the dogmatic kind. There was a hotel in Paris that she used to visit to stay in a room that overlooked the cathedral of Notre-Dame. She would sit in the window for an hour at a time, drinking in the view. The sky held a special attraction for her and she loved to talk about the solar system, the stars and the Milky Way. Deserts, to her mind, were special places with their vastness and mystery. She had spent her honeymoon in Tunisia and travelled in the Middle East when her brother Bohdan was in Amman on a commission for the United Nations to design and construct the modern port of Aqaba in Jordan. On a visit to Morocco, staying in the south of the country on the edge of the Sahara, she had risen early each morning to go to the roof of her hotel and watch the sun rise over the desert. She spoke of many of these things during the evenings she spent by the fire with the boy. On those occasions she was in her element, for each appreciated the other. The age gap became an irrelevance and they shared the same level of curiosity about everything and nothing. The influence she exerted over the boy's life lasted long after she emigrated to the United States.

For many years after she had settled in America, her time with the boy in London continued to be a topic of animated conversation for her. She would embellish her accounts of events in Acton to give them an added dimension, for it was a period of her life like no other. Even after she returned to living at a normal pace, she would revive memories of those days at every opportunity.

Whenever this happened, a special glow came to her face that was never otherwise in evidence. A long time afterwards this benign nostalgia manifested itself more clearly than ever before when the boy confessed to her that the stuff she had once been smoking in the narghile was actually cannabis. The revealing smile that broke out on her face indicated that she had known the fact perfectly well, in those reckless days at Acton, and had resolved not to let on. Ignorance in this case had amounted to utter bliss, so why spoil the fun? Why indeed? It gave the true measure of the woman.

The boy remained in touch with her until she died at the age of ninety-one. Her son Adam afterwards told the boy how, when the hour beckoned, she was staying with her sister-in-law and her niece at Hampton Bays, a seaside resort on Long Island. She had sat up chatting with them late into the Friday evening, but on Saturday morning was heard coughing badly in her bed. When the niece went into the room to see if she was all right, Mrs Rudzka informed her of her impending death. She apologized for causing them so much trouble. A few minutes later she was dead. In her death Mrs Rudzka was as distinguished a human being as she had consistently been throughout her life.

It did not take long for the boy to ask Maria to marry him. When the proposal came out, it was on an impulse; he could not believe he was uttering the words. Maria was still legally under age by the statutes of the day, so she needed to seek her mother's approval. This the mother withheld.

Nothing could persuade her to change her mind, and it seemed that the only way of getting their marriage sanctioned would be to appeal to the courts. When the mother realized they really were prepared to take things that far, she reluctantly agreed for the marriage to go ahead, even though they had no money to speak of. The boy had been through a long period of unemployment and had no savings whatsoever. The only funds they possessed between them was a small nest egg that Maria had managed to put aside in her bank account. She lent the boy £100, which represented a substantial proportion of her savings. This enabled him to order a new suit for his wedding. Apart from that, his total wardrobe consisted of two ill-fitting suits: a navy-blue one, which was tailored, and a grey one, bought off the peg.

Maria's white wedding dress was lovely, and elegant in its simplicity, but as luck would have it, the boy's new suit was not ready in time. He therefore had to make do with being married in his old navy-blue suit, and the saying, 'Necessity is the mother of invention,' was never more true. The suit was put through some skilful restoration work to create the right appearance. The ceremony was held early in 1957 at Brompton Oratory, a large church in South Kensington favoured by the Catholic community. It was a modest affair, attended only by family members and close friends. On Maria's side, the family consisted of her mother, her stepfather and a couple of distant relations. It was impossible for the boy's parents and his three sisters to travel to London for various insurmountable reasons, including those of visa restrictions imposed by the Israeli authorities. The only member of his family to be present was therefore the famous uncle, who also acted as best man. George Hutchinson and his wife Pamela came along, as did the younger members of the Garnett family. Old friends from Battersea Polytechnic turned up in force, along with some new-made friends, but for the boy and Maria the most important guest was Mrs Rudzka. She was beaming as never before and showed by her demeanour that here was a wish come true. The boy had become like an adopted son to her, and the link with a Polish girl was like an added bonus. She could not have dreamed of a better union. The strengthening of the bond through the Polish connection meant a great deal to her. She was truly proud of being Polish and in a way saw Maria as the daughter she had never had. For the married couple, the presence of Mrs Rudzka at their wedding service would for ever be the jewel in the crown of the event, adding to its emotion and happiness, helping to ensure that the pomp and splendour of the biggest society wedding could never outshine its modesty.

Following the wedding service, there was a reception at the Rembrandt Hotel, which lay on the other side of Brompton Road, opposite the Oratory. The boy used what was left over from the £100 to pay for the church and part of the reception. Maria's mother took care of the rest. There was much jollity at the reception, though it remained a low-key affair. Neither bride nor groom wanted any of the long-winded paraphernalia of speech making, with its boring platitudes, that forms such an integral part of the Anglo-Saxon tradition in wedding celebrations. They had seen how this can turn a wedding into a circus, enjoyed only by children and by people who are fond of laughing at their own jokes and having a free binge. With the celebration over, friends and family who attended wished the couple a happy life together and departed. There was no honeymoon. The couple could never have afforded one. The marriage took place on a Saturday and both had to be at their respective jobs the following Monday morning. They were content to celebrate their wedding by going to the cinema to watch a Gary Cooper movie.

Maria's work at the time was with ABC Cinemas, at their headquarters in Soho. She had an allocation of two free cinema tickets a week to see any film of her choice. It was a perk worth having, one that ensured the young couple could have a weekly outing to the pictures. The boy had moved out of Geraldine Road and for their first home together they rented a large room in Clarendon Road in Holland Park, to the east of Notting Hill. One small area of the room was partitioned off and referred to as a kitchenette. It contained a small sink and a gas stove. The lavatory was elsewhere and had to be shared with other tenants, as did the one bathroom. All of that was bad enough in itself, but not so bad as the Irish landlady, Miss Toal, who occupied her own large room on the ground floor and placed hectoring notices all over the house. 'Do not make a noise when climbing the stairs,' was one. Others read: 'When you use the lavatory, do not pull the chain too hard;' 'Be quick when you use the bathroom and don't waste hot water;' and, 'Keep noise to a minimum when you are in your room.' She was an ex-nurse with a sour face and a figure a bit like a bean pole. She was tall, at about five foot ten inches, and extremely thin. She had an anorexic look about her, and her main diet during the week appeared to be nothing more than a bowl of soup and a piece of bread. She had been left the property in the will of one of her rich patients. There was another house in Hampstead that she owned; like the one in Clarendon Road, it was a legacy from a rich patient.

So far as battleaxe landladies were concerned, Miss Toal was the worst example you were likely to come across in a lifetime. Women were her special target. She would set the most outrageous traps to give her an excuse to be as unpleasant to them as she possibly could. As a rampant trouble-maker, she spied on all her lodgers and would poke around in their rooms when they were away or at work. She did this hoping to find something she could bitch about so as to create as much bad feeling as possible. The house telephone, fitted with a pay box, was located directly outside her room on the ground floor. If it rang, she would rush to answer it to ensure no one else got there first. Her reflexes were quick and her agility on such occasions remarkable. She had worked out a system to summon the lodger concerned by means of a bell that was also installed in the corridor directly outside her room. Each lodger had a number of rings allocated to their room. If a certain number of rings sounded, then you knew the call was for you. Once the lodger got to the phone, Miss Toal, of course, could listen in to the whole conversation from behind her closed door. It was a form of social control to ensure good behaviour on the part of all her tenants. The atmosphere in the house was so unpleasant that you hated coming home to it. The only times when its drab and uninviting atmosphere was lifted were on the days when

Miss Toal baked herself a week's supply of bread in one of the basement rooms. On these occasions, a heavenly aroma of freshly baked bread overwhelmed the house and gave it a welcoming feel that it otherwise lacked entirely.

The year 1957 was significant for the boy in another respect, apart from its being the year of his marriage. When his landing restriction had been cancelled by the Home Office a year or so earlier, he had made his application for British citizenship. The process was far from easy in those days; the formalities were rigid and assessing the applicant's background and suitability was undertaken by a division of Scotland Yard. In fact the boy was interviewed twice and given a thorough grilling. The investigators wanted to know everything about him, including his politics and the books he read. They even came to the flat in Clarendon Road and leafed through the books he had in his collection. Although it was all conducted in a relaxed atmosphere, there was a feeling of invasion of privacy that happily does not happen today. Much reform has since been brought in and the procedures have become less intense and more respectful; more tolerant of freedom of choice and of the individual's personal leanings. Finally the grant of British citizenship came through to give the boy a boost in the early stages of his marriage. For the first time in his life he was not a stateless person, but felt a sense of belonging and had a passport to prove it. His Palestinian roots were never to be forgotten: they were deeply embedded in his body and soul; his love for the country of his birth would always remain in parallel with his affection for his newly adopted country.

During the boy and Maria's time of living in Clarendon Road, it had to be admitted that the going was pretty tough in their day-to-day lives. Apart from the situation with the landlady, the boy was badly paid in his job as a junior bank clerk with Crédit Foncier d'Algérie et Tunisie. The job itself was monotonous and did not require much creative input. In those days the French banking system was laborious, the emphasis being on recording each transaction in every way possible. There were ledgers everywhere and a lot of unnecessary time was spent making entries or taking out other entries that were already duplicated in the accounts system. The shuffling of papers was all part of the procedure. It was not easy to follow the system through, except for the old hands, to whom it came naturally as a result of their length of service. The idea behind this method of parallel recording was that it would ensure that no foul play was possible because of the multiplicity of checks at every stage of a transaction. This was questionable. The assumption that the more checks that were built into the system, then the safer it would be, did not ring true in practice. In fact, the more complicated the system, the more opportunities were potentially there to cook the books. Each check relied on the one that came before it; it then went on to reach its final conclusion, often without the least perusal of the original transaction. It was an antiquated system, fallacious and badly in need of reform.

As the boy tussled with the big, heavy-to-lift ledgers, it seemed to him that what he was doing could surely be classified as a menial task. The sheer mechanics of repeating the tiresome activity of entering or taking out entries began to make him feel irritable more often than was good for him. The atmosphere in the bank was also oppressive. Everyone was frightened of losing their job. No allowance was made for latecomers in the mornings, however good or genuine their excuse. Not even train delays or failures were accounted a good enough reason to avoid a reprimand. The same principle applied to those who fell sick and could not possibly come to work. Doctor's certificates were accepted only with reluctance, and on their return to work the patients would be put firmly in the doghouse for several days. Compassion among employers was in severely short supply in those days, and they were generally determined to extract the maximum productivity from their employees. Working hours were also much longer than they are today, and weekends were shorter by reason of employees having to work Saturday mornings. Going away for the weekend could hardly be contemplated: it was too short a break to make it worth while.

The shops were all closed on Sundays, so Saturday afternoons were earmarked as the only time for shopping for essential supplies. What remained of the weekend the boy normally devoted to writing letters on a portable typewriter, which he had bought during his time at Acton. Maria was a more proficient typist than he was, and did the job more quickly and precisely, so she took the task over. Most of these letters were addressed to major UK companies, enquiring about jobs. The boy was adamant that he must find a better paid job that had more prospects than the one at the French bank. To achieve this end, he would have been prepared to live anywhere abroad, whatever hardships this might have entailed at the outset. But out of his applications to over thirty companies, he received only one reply inviting him to come for an interview. This he did readily.

The result was a disappointment, to put it mildly. For one thing, the proposal reeked of racist bigotry. He was offered a job abroad on the understanding that, once he was there, he would be treated as a local employee. The disgraceful proposition staggered him; it had all the marks of blatant discrimination. He could never have envisaged that he would encounter such a dreadful policy when he was a British subject already and had every reason to expect to be treated as one, not as a second-class citizen. The experience left him so disgusted that he never again made an application for any job and resolved to stay put with the French bank till the right opportunity presented itself. The disciplined grind of his work as a ledger clerk would also help him to purge his mind of that type of ugly prejudice, which carried the danger of leaving only bitterness in its wake.

A more flattering possibility had come about during his first week of employment with the French bank. There was an unexpected phone call from the film agent with the parrot. There had been no contact between them for months, but she said she wanted to find out how the boy was and whether he would be available for an important film role. The director of the film himself had seen the boy's photograph on the agent's wall advertising him as an available artist, and insisted that his face suited the part he had in mind. In his view, he had the very strong features that the character demanded. The boy was both flattered and perplexed. Here he was, newly married and with no other means of support than his meagre wages as a junior office clerk. In combination with Maria's earnings, they added up to enough of a joint income to keep body and soul together. The boring and steady job at least paid the rent. Nevertheless he felt he had to think about the amazing offer seriously.

He kept asking himself whether he should seize this unique opportunity and risk losing his only security. It was a most agonizing dilemma to grapple with. On the one hand, he had taken on responsibilities and must live up to them. On the other, there was the lure of stardom and fame – possibilities perhaps within his reach. It was a wonderful thought, but there could be no guarantee that he would be a success in the highly competitive medium of films. In the end, with a heavy heart, he turned the offer down. Afterwards he often asked himself whether it had been the right decision – to opt for security against the exciting hazards of a glamorous career. It was like watching a game of roulette when the croupier swings the wheel of fortune and declares, 'Les jeux sont fait, rien ne va plus.' So it was with the boy. Another career, another life altogether, had beckoned; the door, once closed, would not reopen in the foreseeable future.

Lunch hours at the bank provided a welcome escape from the tedium of ledger work. He would grab a sandwich and during the summer months go and sit on a bench on a bomb site near Bishopsgate that had temporarily been turned into a small garden for the recreation of the public. It was the fashion at the time for women to knit their own jumpers and cardigans. At home he watched Maria doing this in the evenings, and became familiar with the language, reciting the knitter's mantras to produce rows of plain and purl to make a simple pattern and repeating the variations for cable stitch, moss stitch or rib stitch as if he had been doing the knitting himself. It came in useful when he pursued his favourite lunchtime diversion of playing Jack the Lad and chatting up the office girls. They became very animated and intrigued as soon as he showed a knowledgeable interest in their knitting projects. The boy was able to attribute the various flirtatious rendezvous that followed to his superficial vocabulary relating to the craft. And since he never possessed a wedding ring, for he could not afford one at the time, he was happy not to be advertising his status as a married man. It only went to show that poverty could have its advantages.

Back at Clarendon Road there were jollier and more relaxed times when the boy used the typewriter to write all sorts of letters to family and friends abroad. He even wrote to his favourite actor, Marlon Brando. Somewhere he had read that Brando was a keen player of African drums as a hobby; it helped him to switch off during the busy schedules of filming. In his letter, the boy told Brando how he, too, was keen on African drums and sometimes practised them late into the night, especially when he had had a few drinks and smoked a reefer or two in the company of liberated women. The statement was true up to a point; it was the kind of thing he had got up to during his wild days in Acton, when he had produced some rhythmic noises that he claimed to be African, though they never had the resonance of true African music. The Irish landlady in Clarendon Road would never have tolerated bongo drums, of course, and Brando never replied. No doubt he dismissed the letter as having come from a lunatic. Nineteen years later, fate, in one of the rather extraordinary and bizarre games it likes to play, would put another spin on this story.

Out of the blue the boy (by then grown into a business figure who was no stranger to the film industry) found himself in a warm and understanding link-up with the famous actor, who had heard that he also had important connections with the financial world. There followed a regular exchange of transatlantic telephone calls, telexes and letters. Brando's plan was to set up a television series on the plight of the North American Indians and he needed extra finance to do it. His proposal was that if, in return for participation in the project, a large proportion of the finance would come from the Middle East, then he would make his services available to champion the plight of the Palestinians in their search for an identity through statehood. In Brando's view, the twin themes had the potential to make 'exciting programmes from a dramatic point of view' and would serve 'to inform people who are remarkably ignorant about both subjects'. In the event, neither project ever materialized. The idealistic schemes were deemed to be commercially unattractive by the hard-headed financiers; the subjects were too controversial for the major distributors to think of taking them on board. But Brando, unlike some of the characters he played in his films, was highly articulate and had a blazing fire in his belly when it came to the underdog. During their brief association, the businessman was too coy ever to mention the letter he had written as the boy and sent to Brando nineteen years earlier.

The boy and Maria were able to create other diversions in Clarendon Road, to take their minds off the onerous living conditions. On some evenings during the week the boy undertook to give French lessons to Maria, in which they were joined by Pamela, the wife of his friend George Hutchinson, and Emma, the daughter of Maria's dressmaker, who lived in the heart of Soho. To begin with the lessons were taken seriously. Attendance was regular and on time, and some progress was made. But the initial enthusiasm slowly evaporated and the sessions turned into something more like social occasions than exercises in linguistics. At least the whole exercise helped the boy to brush up on his French, which he seldom had the chance to use at the time, and he and his pupils derived some benefits, even if they were not the ones intended at the outset.

All in all, the house in Clarendon Road was one in which the boy and Maria found luck was against them. One Easter they both fell victim to a high fever. Maria became so bad that she had to be taken to hospital in the middle of the night. The boy's condition was not considered to be so serious, so he was left on his own to cope with it as best he could in the dreariness of the rented room. Maria was kept in hospital for ten days before she was allowed home again. A few weeks later the boy was diagnosed as having a fistula. It was deep and nasty and required immediate surgery to avert the danger of peritonitis. He was taken off to St Bartholomew's Hospital at Smithfield for a stay that lasted six weeks.

The operation was not an easy one. It was performed by one of the leading surgeons of the day, and the aftermath was extremely painful because the fistula was in such a delicate place. After the lesion had been scooped out, the wound then had to be allowed to heal by growing new flesh from the inside out so as to fill the cavity left by the operation. The wound needed to be bathed in water three times a day to speed the healing process. Getting through the nights became a traumatic process. He had to sleep resting his rear end on a rubber ring to avoid any undue pressure on the wound. The nights were long and the boy could only sleep when sheer exhaustion finally forced him into unconsciousness for a few precious hours.

The nurses were kind and helpful, and inevitably the boy had his favourite among them. She was called Rosie and spoilt him silly. It fell to Rosie to have to perform some unpleasant tasks to ensure that the healing did not block the back passage. As she carried these out, the boy screamed with the excruciating pain, but afterwards he would joke with her about how he could never entertain the idea of having a homosexual relationship. Rosie was a brunette with short hair, a tall, good-looking girl in her early twenties who was handsome rather than pretty. Her face possessed a welcoming quality of rare freshness, as of an English rose that has been sheltered from the sun and the harsher aspects of the English climate. She treated the boy with special care and attention, realizing that besides suffering physical pain, he was feeling crushed and shattered by the hospital's stern and clinical regime. He was often in low spirits and badly in need of someone able to give his morale a lift and ease him towards recovery.

The boy responded to Rosie's kindness with heartfelt expressions of poetic gratitude. At times these took the form of a flirtatious banter that unwittingly masked a more serious undercurrent. He never allowed himself to admit it, but he had developed a crush on Rosie that helped to lift his spirits, despite the bodily discomforts he was enduring in the aftermath of what had been a difficult and complex piece of surgery. Maria plainly observed his obsessive fondness for the nurse when she came to visit, and used to tease him about it. He went on the defensive on such occasions and would never come clean about his real underlying feelings for Rosie, though he could never stop himself singing her praises as his Angel of Mercy, without whom his ordeal would have been so much worse.

Maria's playful observations had a ring of truth to them. The boy's vulnerability in his hospital circumstances meant that he would, as a reflex, reach out emotionally to any woman who was able to show him tenderness and dedication beyond the call of duty. In these things, human beings display their kinship with their domestic animal companions, for they too will reach out lovingly to those who give them warmth, who feed and care for them. Rosie bathed his tender wound twice a day, changed his dressings at the same time, and performed delicate and painful tasks that required the boy to be totally relaxed. Because of all these things, his attachment to Rosie grew. When she was away for her day off or busy on another ward, he sank into gloom and a feeling of being forsaken. In his eyes, no other nurse could be a substitute for Rosie or begin to match her nursing skills. Her tender hands alleviated his pain and gave him unshakeable confidence in the belief that everything she did for him was for his own good. It was like a form of hypnosis that anaesthetized his senses and made the agonies of his treatment tolerable during his time in hospital. The rapport and chemistry that was there between him and Rosie was only there, he could think, through divine dispensation and grace.

The soft spot he had for Rosie must also, he reflected, have something to do with when he was living at Acton in Mrs Rudzka's house. At that time he had stumbled on a date with a delightfully attractive young nurse who was training at Hackney's general hospital. They had hit it off at once and progressed in their relationship to becoming good friends once the physical attraction started to wane. She had then proceeded to introduce him to a whole host of her fellow nurses, with the result that there was almost a surfeit of them, taking turns to visit the boy at regular intervals. Subsequently they formed an alliance designed to promote a bohemian philosophy of pursuing high jinks and living on the edge. Nurses in general are perceived as having few inhibitions and to be well versed in sexual exploits as a result of their medical environment and training, involving exposure to the normally hidden and intimate parts of the anatomy.

It had been the nurses who had provided the boy with the lumps of medical charcoal he had heated over a gas ring and used in the narghile when smoking cannabis. Now that the boy was married and reformed, at least to a degree, the memories of his past life seemed to hover around him enticingly at times. Despite the change in his personal status, the link between past and present remained heavily entrenched in his psyche and the connecting currents went on exerting an influence on his behaviour. He needed them as worthy reminders of how he had evolved, the lessons that had been learned and the fulfilments that were to be cherished. In essence it explained one of the elements that gave him a bond with Rosie for the duration of his stay in hospital, for she was the nurse who somehow embodied the nursing myth that the boy cultivated in his own mind. It was idealistic in concept, but in reality very much down to earth.

When Maria came to visit the boy in Bart's, every evening after work, it was she who bore the brunt of his frustrations, for he was not always in a good mood. She could not avoid feeling lonely and tired. Being at work all day, then having to rush to the hospital every evening, caused her a great deal of stress. The way Maria coped during that period was a testimony to her commitment to her man. Her resilience knew no bounds. She demonstrated how she could be, in adversity, equal to the best of them. She also had to contend with the busybody of a landlady.

When the boy was admitted to St Bartholomew's, Miss Toal had made herself very nice to him within her own narrow understanding of niceness, but Maria, left vulnerable and defenceless on her own in the house, became fair game for her beastliness. One night, when Maria returned home after visiting the boy in hospital, she found Miss Toal had placed ten chairs round the walls of their room. All the chairs were badly in need of repair and their imposition in the room gave it the look of a storage unit in a warehouse. Three days after depositing the chairs, Miss Toal accosted

Maria one evening and accused her of jumping up and down on their seats to cause the maximum damage; it had been done, she asserted, as an act of retaliation against herself. The accusation was outrageous, a fabrication to enable Miss Toal to traumatize poor Maria, who had enough troubles at the time and had already received more than her fair share of Miss Toal's persecutions.

The boy, when he finally returned home from St Bartholomew's, found Miss Toal waiting to greet him, beaming with joy. She warmly shook his hands and told him how she had prayed for his full recovery throughout his time in hospital; how she thanked the Lord for heeding her prayers. Then, in a rare moment of contrition, she admitted to the boy that she had falsely accused Maria of damaging the chairs she had placed in their care. Now she accepted the error of her judgement. As a result, she had gone to confession, for she was a devout Catholic, and had cleansed her soul and felt the better for it. The Good Lord, in His mercy, had forgiven her. Those were her last words on the subject.

While the boy's stay in hospital had continued, the length of time it was taking began to make his prospects at the bank look bleak. The bank manager was a hard taskmaster. He used to stand at his office door each morning so he could fix any latecomer with a look that conveyed the stern warning that the sack was likely to be on the cards. He would admonish an employee for any minor infringement of the rules, and he enforced his rigid style of discipline with an obvious relish. He would make enquiries about what progress the boy was making in hospital, but there was more of a threat implied than any kindness or concern about the illness. He urged that the boy ought to be thinking about his future and his responsibilities as a married man. All of this made the boy feel nervous; indirectly, it may have impeded the healing process. In the late 1950s, finding a job with secure prospects and a reasonable salary was not easy. Choice was not readily available as a commodity. And the boy was not in a league where he could exert influence or pull strings with those who had it.

He was helpless to alter anything in his present situation. All he could do was try to blot out the notion that he might, through his illness, find himself once again unemployed. But at last he reached a point where he began to feel better; the wound was starting to heal without any complications. He heaved a sigh of relief when he was released from hospital, though they told him he must go on receiving treatment and attending the outpatients department. Now it was Maria who had to take over some of Rosie's tasks. The dressings still needed to be changed twice a day. Maria had to clean the wound thoroughly and apply some ointment to assist the mending process, but the most effective way by far of ensuring there was slow but steady progress was to bathe it as much as possible, for water is the best healing agent known in nature. Maria also discovered that sanitary towels made the most effective form of dressing in this particular case. Her improvisation won the full approval of Bart's outpatients staff, who readily proclaimed it a good idea. The boy was consumed with embarrassment, and kept the story of the sanitary towels a secret, fearing he would be teased mercilessly by his male friends if they ever got wind of it.

It was a long time before full recovery was achieved and these procedures could be dispensed with, but at least life had begun to move on again. The boy and Maria had no wish to go on living in the room in Clarendon Road for longer than was necessary. They managed to find a small flat near by in Royal Crescent, and prepared to move into their second home together.

Among the boy's valued friendships, the one with Miss Willmott – who had been his first friend in England – was no longer the same after his marriage. They were still close, but the closeness took on a different quality. It was less free and more restrained. The very fact of Miss Willmott's disability meant that her relationships with men were in one way very restricted. She had never had a boyfriend in the traditional sense of the word, nor as far as he knew had she ever had a physical relationship with anyone of either sex. She felt that her place lay to one side of the mainstream of society, from where she could observe what went on without being a participant. All of this notwithstanding, she definitely preferred the company of men. She had to work mainly with women, though she could never feel relaxed in their company. Her kindness knew no bounds, and in her charitable work nothing stood in the way of her achieving her goal. Yet the fact remained that she loved men but merely tolerated women.

When the boy introduced her to Maria, she was very pleased that there was now a woman who could take over some of those responsibilities that she felt she had had to shoulder when the boy was in her care. Her relationship with him became something more akin to that with the blind man. The blind man had his wife; so, too, did the boy now have his wife. It was not that Miss Willmott resented the wives, though in a way they intruded into her territory. It was more that she was resigned to them, and her resignation had a very gracious quality indeed.

With her retirement, she grew contented with her familiar surroundings in the borough of Streatham and focused her energies more and more on charitable work within her parish. Eventually she lost contact with Miss Newton, who left London to go and live in the country. For the boy, it seemed that an era in his life had passed. He retained fond memories of those two ladies who had, in their own way, done so much to shape his early life in Britain. He owed them both a heavy debt of gratitude.

He saw Miss Willmott on two more occasions before she died. Many years after her death, he learnt that in her will she had left him a large oil painting of an Arabian scene. Unfortunately her executors had been unable to trace his whereabouts and so had put the painting up for auction and donated the proceeds to charity. He felt sad when he heard about it. The picture was a gift he would have loved to possess, not for any monetary value it may have held, but as a reminder of all the hospitality, kindness and friendship Miss Willmott had shown him.

At the time the boy and Maria moved to Royal Crescent, the uncle finally took the decision to sell the house in Geraldine Road. As a fully fledged engineer with his hard-won degree from Battersea Polytechnic, he felt secure enough in his job with the General Electric Company in Birmingham to pull up his London roots and make a life elsewhere. He made a good profit from the sale of the house. The original purchase had only been possible through the loan of £1,000, secured from Papp Garnett with the help of the boy. The loan was in due course repaid out of the rents the uncle collected from his friend Stinous, as well as the boy and the sitting tenants in the basement and on the ground floor. One of the odd things in families, when it comes to money, is the way it can lead to the some of the most treasured loyalties being cast aside, sometimes unwittingly. Dissension and enmity can become entrenched, even in families, through financial disagreements. The uncle never offered the boy any share of the profit he had made. In all probability, the boy would have declined the offer, but the gesture would have been appreciated, given the provenance of the loan and other relevant factors. On the contrary, some years later the uncle unleashed a fit of bitterness when he claimed that the boy still owed him rent from the time when his student's allowance from home was stopped by political circumstances. But time is a big healer in all these matters. The boy soon forgot the insensitivity of his uncle's claim, even though he had to pay it by instalments just to preserve family solidarity.

Most people remember incidents where they felt themselves to be the victim of ill will, yet forget other acts of good will that have been shown to them. The uncle had his idiosyncrasies, but at heart he was a kind and helpful man who had had to put up with various unbearable pressures created by the boy's devilment and unreasonable behaviour. Whenever there was a major commotion or disruption at Battersea Polytechnic, the boy was invariably the moving force behind it and the uncle felt responsible. He was overcome with shame on the numerous occasions when he was told how the culprit was his nephew. Blood ties are important in the culture of the Middle East, and any disgrace that descends on one member of a family is felt to reflect shame on all the others. The uncle tried desperately to tame the boy, but the task proved impossible. It was as if the boy's demons were out of control, and there was nothing the uncle could do except cringe and bear the circumstances.

In an attempt to win sympathy for his predicament, the uncle would regale any company with an account of the latest incident that had caused him immeasurable grief; such as the evening, during a party at the polytechnic, when the boy was in a ribald mood after a few drinks and attempted, in front of everyone, to disrobe a pretty, vivacious girl for the fun of it. The worst of it was that the girl, far from being indignant at this treatment, didn't seem to mind at all, but thought it cool and hip, as if she was playing a part in one of the 'new wave' movies of the time. And then the boy had an urge to round off the evening on a dramatic note. On his way home with various members of his gang, he smashed a glass panel at a bus stop with his bare fist. Naturally this act of bravado left him covered in blood, but he nonchalantly bandaged the hand with his handkerchief and paid no more attention to it.

The uncle was completely unable to fathom what had happened to the boy to turn him into this unpredictable youth who was capable of all sorts of aberrations. As a small child back home, he had been frail, shy and rather cuddly. The mature female members of his family had all petted and pampered him as if he had been breast-fed and hand-raised by each one of them. Even women friends of the family would never lose the opportunity to take him to bed in the afternoon during siesta time, so they could snuggle his tiny head to their breast to make him feel the particular warmth that only the female of the species can impart. There was no need to look further for the reasons why the boy always felt such a close affinity with women. It originated from the closeness to the female body he experienced from his earliest years. The very smell of a woman was more nourishing to him than his mother's milk; it was like nectar from the beyond. This kind of nurturing had left him with a sense of adoration for women. In many respects, he considered them superior to men. They were God's masterly creation, he used to say, especially at times when he was totally enveloped in the soft folds of the female form. Yet the boy's evolution from loving child to wayward prankster, intent on causing havoc on the slightest whim, was a mystery beyond the uncle's abilities to solve. Nevertheless, despite the boy's failings and the torment he caused him, the uncle secretly admired him for his *savoir vivre*; a quality he completely lacked in his own personality and perhaps wished he could have had himself.

The flat in Royal Crescent was again lacking in its own bathroom. Again there was a lavatory that had to be shared – this time with a single girl who lived on the floor above. The landlord was called John Kirby, a cockney born and bred. He was a likeable rogue with shady connections. Most of the time he was entertaining to deal with, so long as you realized he was strictly not to be trusted. At other times he betrayed signs of meanness, such as rigging the gas meters during the winter months so he could extract more money from his tenants. Often he would redeem himself by unexpected acts of kindness. He had managed to avoid being conscripted into the war and had remained in London during the blitz, much involved in the black market. It was a career that had provided him with a lucrative living. Subsequently he owned property in Soho and a nightclub as well as the house in Royal Crescent. His vocation was trading at every level. The size of a transaction was not his primary concern; he would buy and sell anything so long as he saw the chance of showing a return. The process interested him far more than the amount of profit to be derived.

John had never married, though throughout his life he had a string of women in tow. His taste in that department might best be described as 'accommodating'. He practised the adage that 'variety is the spice of life', and one of his favourite remarks was, 'A woman is a woman.' He led a bawdy sort of life that revolved round drinking and smoking, both of which he considered necessary evils; the women he saw as a decoration and a challenge. He liked nothing better than to play off one woman against another, then sit back and watch the carnage. To have women fighting over him, he once confided to the boy, was even better than sex. It had more of an erotic charge and held out much greater promise of fulfilment. Shortly before Maria and the boy moved to Royal Crescent, there had been a very posh girlfriend unlike any other in his life. She was accustomed to high living as the wife of the managing director of a famous London store. Her stepdaughter was the girl in the top flat with whom Maria and the boy had to share the bathroom. The stepmother was an attractive woman who was always chic in appearance, and John described the relationship as a union of opposites. While she 'liked a bit of rough', he would say glibly, he enjoyed screwing a woman above his station. In this he displayed a parallel attitude to the trendy intelligentsia, a majority of whom think left and sleep right.

John's live-in woman provided a study in contrasts. She was called Nita, a publican who looked the part: a large lady with big bosoms. What John saw in her was not immediately apparent. Perhaps she was a whore in bed. That apart, she drank too much and her face was always bloated. The vulgarity of her speech was geared up to the level of drunks and bar flies. Nita was subservient to John's every need, yet expected to receive his full attention at all times. This made her very possessive of her man, and she resented anyone who grew too close to him. John was not by nature the sort to be beholden to anyone. As a master of intrigue, he loved winding people up, especially those who made easy prey. Nita was one such. She could also be very moody. At times it was impossible to fathom any reason for her displeasure or lack of warmth. There were days when she would hardly acknowledge the existence of anyone else in the house and push past you on the stairs or in the hall without uttering a word. It was as if you were a total stranger, or non-existent. All in all, she was a woman of no substance herself, and she contributed nothing to the congeniality of her surroundings.

Nita notwithstanding, life became much happier and

more eventful for the boy and Maria after their move to Royal Crescent. They settled in, helped by the fact that they already knew a few people living in the area. George and Pamela Hutchinson had their home within walking distance, and another well-known journalist, Peter Hedden Knight, and his wife Joanna also lived near by. They made up a group who met up regularly at the Mitre, a pub in Holland Park Avenue, mostly at weekends. Their friendship was so close that the Knights hosted a birthday party for Maria at their home in Ladbroke Road. Peter Knight was head of the Arab News Bureau in London, so he also had strong links with the Middle East. Among his friends was Emile Bustani, the Lebanese contractor and distinguished politician, who had various connections within the United Kingdom, his circle of acquaintance including members of Parliament and the House of Lords. Bustani maintained a permanent suite at the Hyde Park Hotel in Knightsbridge, where he was privileged to be able to keep his own furniture. George Hutchinson also knew Bustani and wanted the boy to meet him. The boy was to see at first hand how this charismatic Lebanese politician could hold people under his spell. Bustani was generously impulsive and gave George the cashmere cardigan he was wearing simply because George had admired it. George was simply not given the option to refuse the gift. He left with the cardigan, feeling both enriched and pampered. When Bustani died in a plane crash in the sea off Beirut a few years later, he was a great loss to his country. He was a Maronite Christian, but in all his business enterprises he chose his employees according to merit not by sectarian allegiance.

Things were beginning to look up on all fronts in the

life of the boy and Maria, who had been promoted to a better job: she was now in charge of a pool of girls and her stature grew with the responsibility. The boy was making good progress in his work at the bank and was even beginning to like it. In their spare time they also did some trading on the side. They went along to the Portobello Antique Market to buy bits and pieces and then sold them together with other items obtained from their landlord, John Kirby, who had the spirit of barter in his blood. John would have swindled his own grandmother given the chance, and he could not be watched too carefully. If they managed to get the better of him, it happened less often than the other way round. But it was all done in a good spirit and the three of them got a kick from playing the game.

The young couple were always looking for ways and means to augment their salaries, which were at a similar level: about £7 10s. (£7.50) a week each: average earnings then for a young person. They would jump at any opportunity. When the cleaning lady was ill, they volunteered to take it in turns to clean the stairs from top to bottom for 5s. (25p). When George and Pamela needed their bathroom redecorating in Holland Park, they offered to do the job cheaply, and did it well and in the time specified. The boy and Maria were alike in being ambitious to improve their living standards. They aimed to get the best they could afford and had no interest in accumulating money for its own sake.

Maria developed a passion for the small items of antique jewellery that she bought and sold, aided and abetted by John Kirby, who was every bit as passionate. He took

Maria under his wing for love of the bartering that went on between them. They haggled over prices for hours and traded and bartered non-stop. As they sold each other small choice pieces, it had to be admitted it was normally a one-way traffic, except for a few occasions. Maria ended up owing him money on a more or less permanent basis, which she paid him back weekly on the never-never principle. But the maximum outlay was never more than 2s. (20p). Nita did not like the various concessions that Maria was able to wheedle out of John and she often accused him of having a soft spot for Maria in his transactions with her. In general all parties managed to maintain an *entente cordiale* on the surface, but underneath resentment seethed. When it came to it, Nita was afraid of alienating John to the point where she would lose him. If she ever began to cause trouble, John would start to call her names and peace would be restored, even though he had probably been partly responsible for any bout of jealousy in the first place. John was a larger-than-life character who lived intemperately, indulged himself and sometimes the women around him, and could not give a damn for any other consideration.

For the boy and Maria the pattern for their evenings began when whoever arrived home first from work started to prepare their meal. They had to improvise a lot. They could not afford expensive cuts from the butcher's shop, but instead bought mince, which they cooked in the oven with fresh onions and tinned tomatoes, usually serving this up with a few steamed potatoes. At other times they bought a couple of pieces of chicken to roast with some potatoes; or they cooked spaghetti or had cold ham garnished with lettuce or tomato salad. Steamed rice with cooked beans was an occasional treat. They were usually famished after a day at work and never suffered from lack of appetite.

After eating dinner, they went out to walk hand in hand along Holland Park Avenue. When it was dark they enjoyed gazing into the brightly lit windows of the rich and famous, the area having always been known for its affluence. Maria was mainly interested in seeing the contents of the houses, for she was endowed with a sharp eye for the style and colour of their interior design. The boy also got excited by what they saw, though in his case he was more preoccupied with the dream of one day securing something similar for themselves. At this time in his life he was a dreamer who enjoyed the dream more often than the reality. He was content to bask in the glory of what might be and built around himself a world of make believe that kept his spirits high. Maria was much more down to earth and very cautious about the future. She was far less prone to fantasy and her clear-eyed sense of perspective acted as a counter-balance.

Once, when they saw a parked Rolls-Royce, the boy pointed to it with the remark that his would be a different colour and have a longer base. It would be custom-made to his own specifications and contain a small bar. Then the Princess (meaning Maria) would ride in it to film premières like any Hollywood star. At this point in his ravings Maria would tell him to shut up and stop dreaming. The boy was feeling especially rich on that particular day. He had just received a cheque for £10 from the *Evening Standard*. This came about through a casual remark he made to George Hutchinson about having received a postcard from Cairo, with the inscription in Arabic on the stamp reading, 'Egypt, the tomb of the invaders' – a reference to the recent Suez Crisis. The stamp was reproduced in the 'Londoner's Diary' column and the cheque was in payment for the contribution from the boy. It had put him into a boisterous mood and he was seeing the world through glasses tinted with pure gold dust.

Back in the Holy Land, the boy's father had retired from his job with Barclays Bank in Haifa. He had stopped work at the age of fifty-three. His complaint had been that the job became untenable following the change of regime; he could no longer recognize or relate to the banking sector in the state of Israel. Early retirement meant accepting a much reduced pension, and this did little to help matters at the time. He had no other source of income and very few savings. The pension in itself was adequate for life's basic necessities, but there was no flexibility to allow him to carry on adding to his modest art collection. On the social side, with so many of the people he knew having left the country, he found himself isolated and at a loose end. This left him with nothing better to do than be an ogre in his own home. With his constant interference in the running of the household, he made life intolerable for all other family members.

His eldest daughter was fortunate enough to have been able to leave for Lebanon with her carpenter husband. The next youngest daughter, who accompanied her, became established as a senior secretary at the British Embassy in Beirut. This left the youngest daughter of all, who was the baby of the family and her father's favourite, as the only one of the children still in the family home. The boy in London and his three sisters all communicated with each other by letter. In this way they were able somehow to reconcile themselves to being so widely dispersed. As they adapted to their new ways of life, they managed to keep in touch and maintain their family bond as best as they could. Throughout, the boy's mother continued to fulfil her role as faithful servant of her husband. She never flinched from performing her duties in the most trying circumstances, especially those caused by her husband's sudden retirement. She had endured enough while he was still at work, but now she found the strain of having him around all day was nearly too much for her and it was driving her mad. In the end, as she did with everything else, she got used to the situation and seemed to cope with it. How she was able to keep her wits about her astonished everyone who knew her and her family, but at least she had the unfailing support of her youngest daughter, who had found a job in Haifa at the British Consulate. This was located conveniently only a few yards from the house. The daughter was even able to go home during her coffee breaks to check that all was well. It was a very relaxed job and she missed it during the weekends when she had to stay at home the whole time.

In the letters the boy received from his youngest sister, she told him about the Ryecarts, a husband and wife with two sons who had become neighbours and who had befriended their parents. Mr Ryecart was the Anglican vicar to the British compound. He was kind and considerate, with no pretensions whatsoever. He performed his clerical duties with great piety, yet remained the sort of man who kept both feet squarely on the ground. He was always available to anyone in trouble and never missed an opportunity to help the needy or any who sought his counsel. His well-developed sense of humour endeared him to his flock. Among those who had the privilege to meet him, there was none who would speak ill of him. On the contrary, he was revered and appreciated as few other vicars can ever have been.

His wife, Vera, came from an aristocratic Austrian family and owned a large castle in her country of origin. Her friendliness reached out to everyone and she bubbled with good humour no matter what the occasion. Her demeanour inspired a warmth of feeling that captivated everyone with whom she came into contact. She never ran short of words, composed limericks in English and generally gushed with mirth. In other words, she in no way matched the stereotypical image of a vicar's wife. Wherever she went, it was her unusual personality and her ability to make herself at home anywhere that drew others to her in a unique way and made her popularity unassailable. So far as the Ryecarts were concerned, the healing gift of laughter was as important a part of their ministry as any theological precepts.

When the Ryecarts took up the appointment to the English community in the Holy Land in 1950, the elder of their two sons was back home at boarding school in Britain. Their younger son, Patrick, however, was still only two years old. The boy's sister described in her letters how Patrick would be brought, in his very tiny bed, to be looked after by their parents while the Ryecarts were touring in the country on pastoral duties. In fact Patrick virtually grew up, till the age of six, with the boy's youngest sister. At the time when Maria and the boy were married, Patrick had also come to England to go to boarding school, though they still only heard about each other at one remove. They were destined never to meet until many years later, when Patrick was already an established actor; and then they wished they could have met him earlier, when he was still in boarding school. This turn of events was brought about when the boy became a theatrical producer, in conjunction with his friend, Howard Panter, to present a dramatization of J. P. Donleavy's novel *The Beastly Beatitudes of Balthazar B* at the Duke of York's Theatre in London. The leading actors in the play were Simon Callow and Patrick Ryecart.

The boy's job in the bank became more secure. The work he was undertaking started to be more interesting. He began to grasp the basic elements of banking; and in the absence of never having seriously tried anything else, he was even growing to like it. Additional responsibilities brought with them rises in salary and he realized he must just bide his time. The real break would come along when destiny was ready. Life in Royal Crescent also moved at a steadier pace. The boy and Maria saw their circle of friends and acquaintances slowly widen. They began to appreciate their new way of life. Invitations to social events became more frequent and they found themselves building a popularity within the widened circle. There were other old friends whom they missed. Mrs Rudzka and her son

Adam had decided that their new life was definitely in America and taken the decision to sell the Acton house. The friends who had made up the gang at the Battersea Polytechnic were either scattered all over the country or had joined the army and been posted abroad. Everyone must move on in life and follow their own path; in time the former common ground with contemporaries loses its solidity and slips away. It is a normal pattern for friendships to form, change and dissolve.

Making friendships within the Middle Eastern enclaves in London was not an easy option in the late 1950s. The Arab community was not as widespread as it has subsequently become and its various national groups tended to keep themselves to themselves. They circulated little and the chances of meeting an Arab socially were minimal. One evening, however, Maria and the boy went to a cocktail party at the invitation of a former Iraqi journalist who was starting to dabble in real estate. A charming young couple came up and introduced themselves. The man was called Hilal, and he was, like the boy, married to a Polish girl. He was handsome, with the aristocratic looks of a desert sheik. Her name was Teresa, and while she was attractive, her curvaceous body hinted at the temptations of a rich diet and a tendency to put on weight through lack of exercise. These first impressions turned out to be accurate as they came to know them better.

Hilal was the son of an Iraqi tribal leader who was also a well-known figure in European society. He had an assured, imposing manner that made him stand out in any group: always in control of the situation and priding himself on his heritage. He never missed an opportunity to talk about his tribe, their ways and customs and the traditions of chivalry for which they were renowned. A tribal society, he often remarked, needed to operate by its own rules, however harsh these might sometimes seem to outsiders. Questions of honour and gallantry were paramount in every decision that was taken. His family must have been very wealthy to judge by his own lifestyle, which was extravagant even by later standards, when the austerity of the post-war years had finally lifted. He did not need to work for a living, which meant he had no real commitments or pressures on his time. In effect, he was invariably at a loose end and liked to use his leisure finding ways of diverting his friends. He was a generous and amiable host who never allowed any of the intimates in his circle to dig into their own pockets and extended this largesse to anyone he happened to meet.

Maria and the boy much enjoyed making the acquaintance of Teresa and Hilal, and although they never set out to take advantage of his habitual generosity, they appreciated the chance to dine at some of the best places in London, and they discovered there was something deeply satisfying about the new-found social mobility that followed. Among Hilal's many gifts was a jumper of vicuña wool for Maria. It had been given to him by his father, who bought it at a famous shop in Bond Street called Sulka. It was of such quality that Maria was still wearing it over forty years later. The boy and Hilal also discovered that they shared a common interest in photography. The boy had become a keen photographer. Although he could not afford an expensive camera, he managed to buy a second-hand German Voigtlander manufactured in the 1930s. It was basic in every sense, but it managed to do the task required of it.

The boy had had his camera with him on the Île du Levant, the nudist island, and taken some remarkable photographs of bare human flesh *en masse* as the naturists circulated or stretched themselves out in the burning sun. Then, during his stay with Mrs Rudzka, he indulged his enthusiasm for photography by photographing any girlfriend who was willing to expose her body, sometimes for art's sake or more often to create an erotic atmosphere as an overture to other more pleasurable activities.

One day, when Hilal and Teresa visited Royal Crescent, Hilal asked the boy to show him his album of photographs. As Teresa and Maria got down to chatting in the background, the two men started to turn the pages together. Then an odd thing happened. Hilal's eyes became riveted on the picture of one outstandingly attractive young woman. She stood out from all the rest for the quality of her features and her amazing figure. Hilal seemed stunned and there was a long silence. As the boy tried to lead him on through the album, he kept coming back to the one picture, as if in the grip of a sudden bizarre obsession. Totally mesmerized by the photograph, he asked the boy for the girl's identity. The boy, flattered by Hilal's appreciative attention and feeling this must reflect well on his taste in women, launched into a lyrical description of her many physical attributes. As Hilal listened, his face turned ashen. Finally he called Teresa over and asked her to look at the photograph. The boy was baffled by the significance of what was happening as Hilal asked Teresa whether she recognized the woman. She hesitated for a brief moment, as if regaining her composure, and then answered in the affirmative that it was her.

It was the turn of the boy to be stunned as he realized that this Teresa was the same Teresa he had known some years before in a much slimmer version. The transformation was astonishing. She was still only in her middle twenties, was still good looking, but she had lost her figure completely. He had utterly failed to recognize her as the same person. It was down to him to break the embarrassed silence that descended on the room. Thinking very fast, he toned down everything he had just said and tried to put a more detached gloss on the circumstances that led to the picture being taken. It had been a relationship driven by friendship rather than anything else, he insisted, and was all above board.

As he said it, he found himself somehow at a loss to explain why Teresa had not shown any sign of recognizing him before this happened. The boy had hardly changed. Her case was different. Women tend to undergo transformations more easily than men and sometimes even seem to alter personalities with changes of style. Teresa had become an unrecognizable version of her former self, at least as the boy remembered her, and it was within the realm of feasibility that the boy should have failed to relate the old Teresa to the current one. Could she have been aware of the situation, but kept silent so as to bury the glorious past and with it the delectable Teresa who had stood in a league of her own? Was she somehow ashamed of having let herself go and did not want to admit it? These questions raced through the boy's mind without hope of resolution.

Hilal took it all in good part. He made no further mention of the extraordinary coincidence. And the friendship survived. The boy meanwhile felt so embarrassed by the whole episode that he never broached the subject with Teresa, not even at a later date when he happened to be alone with her. He was content to let the conundrum rest. His fear was that if it should be unravelled it might lose its mystique and possibly lead to further confusion. By his reckoning, providence had dealt him a lucky hand on this occasion; it seemed wiser not to tempt fate further. Why venture into unchartered waters for the sheer hell of it?

For the boy, the meeting with Hilal was a prelude to meeting many other Arabs, some of whom would prove instrumental in the boy's rise in business in the years ahead. The contacts he was making in the City through his work at Crédit Foncier d'Algérie et du Tunisie were also going to be important to him in many ways. The bank's situation at Bishopsgate, in the heart of the famous 'square mile', meant that he met many distinguished people who worked there within the world of finance or who happened to be passing through, and all the time he was adding to his growing circle of friends. One such was a stockbroker by the name of Sebastian Wheeler. He and his sister were both particularly kind to the boy, especially during his stay in hospital when he was recovering from his fistula operation. They entertained the boy and Maria at their home in the country and were supportive in the early days of his banking career.

Another young man who befriended them and played a similar role was Francis Ebury, who had recently succeeded to his father's title on the baronet's death and become Lord Ebury. He possessed an enchanting personality and was very warm-hearted and accommodating; what's more he was enlightened in his views. As an aristocrat, who was also heir presumptive to the Earl of Wilton, Francis Ebury provided another object lesson for the boy in the unexpected social ironies of the British class system: he had not a grain of snobbishness in his body. He was simply someone who made it a great joy to be in his company. There was a strange and telling coincidence from the beginning, arising from the fact that he lived next to the Carmelite church just off Kensington High Street. For the boy, this held a special sentimental significance: his home in Haifa had looked on to a magnificent view of the Carmelite church on Mount Carmel. When he was about thirteen, he liked to make his way to the summit of Mount Carmel to visit the monastery and admire the panorama of the bay of Haifa stretching out below.

The presence of the two churches in the two different countries seemed like more than an accidental link. The feelings it engendered stirred again some years later during the course of an encounter that he had with the writer Roald Dahl, when Roald told him how, as a fighter pilot with the RAF during the Second World War, he would regularly fly over Mount Carmel on escort duty for bombing raids against positions of the Vichy government in Lebanon. He shared the boy's sentimental attachment to Mount Carmel, remembering how the Arab peasants on top of the mountain would wave to him and the bomber pilots to wish them safe sorties. Then they would do the same as they returned to welcome them back to base.

When the boy and Maria first met Lord Ebury, he was

distraught at the break-up of his marriage. This did not prevent him showing them a special hospitality and friendship. He was very much into opera, which happened to be an artistic medium that neither of them had as yet discovered. The Carmelites again provided a key theme. He bought and played to them a long-playing record of what was then a brand-new work from the French composer Francis Poulenc: the *Dialogues des Carmélites*. With a libretto based on a play by Georges Bernanos, that was based in turn on other sources, including a chronicle of true events, it told the story of the tribulations of a community of Carmelite nuns who came under persecution during the French Revolution. The opera established the varied characters of the nuns and their struggles to maintain their faith, up till the point where they were condemned to death under the Reign of Terror. The final scene, with its haunting drum strokes as the nuns fell victim to the guillotine one by one, singing the *Salve regina* to the end, was a shattering experience in musical and emotional terms. It was one of those occasions when a work of art has an impact that lasts for life: the power of opera could hardly have been better illustrated. As a listening experience, it provided the seed from which a whole new field of exploration was sown for the boy and Maria. From there on, the love of opera became a consuming passion.

They reciprocated as best they could, inviting Lord Ebury back to their simple lodgings in Royal Crescent so as to introduce him to Middle Eastern cuisine. With an obvious appreciation, he sampled the variety of dishes they had prepared. It was an evening when bread was broken together. In broader terms, this meant that a special bond was established. Only a few months later, Lord Ebury decided he would leave England to go to live in Australia and start a new life there. He was a person of courage and tenacity and his departure left a gap in both business and social circles that was hard to fill. Over the years, the boy and Maria received a couple of postcards from him, and although any direct contact was lost after that, he remained a distant and silent friend. They liked to think of him living on the vast continent he had chosen on the far side of the world, enjoying the freedom to pursue another passion in his life: the study of ornithology. Circumstances may draw people together at certain times, then send them off in divergent directions, but the lasting values of friendship continue to reach across the divides of time and space.

A major incident at work was to bring about a dramatic change in the boy's career. He had been attached to the foreign-exchange department, and in those economically turbulent days it was the hub of the bank's activities. The job demanded a quick mathematical mind as well as a strongly informed insight into the market. Sterling was then a major currency in world trade and, more than that, was accepted internationally as a reserve currency. Because of its unique role, it became a target for speculators worldwide. This caused it to fluctuate sharply; sometimes even to go into free fall. The years of struggle for recovery after the war were made even more difficult by a tendency of British governments to rely on the devaluation mechanism to shore up the national economy. People were therefore always nervous about holding sterling, yet it was a currency that most financial centres of the world dealt in on a very large scale. To relocate it down the line would have had even worse repercussions than devaluation. The dollar was beginning its rise up the scale of prominence, but sterling would still play an important role for years to come.

Against this background, the main foreign-exchange dealer at the bank was taken ill and it seemed he was unlikely to return to his former post in the near future. With the pressure being so intense, the position needed formidable mental strength as well as a firm conviction that the way you were reading the market was on the whole the right one. His doctors confirmed that if he were ever to come back to work, then it was improbable that he would be fit to resume his previous duties. When all this was happening, the boy's task was to record all the foreign-exchange transactions in a ledger and type the confirmation of each one for forwarding to the client concerned. It was a monotonous, automatic task, though the fact that he was doing it would surprisingly pave the way ahead as a test of his abilities and the strength of his mental make-up. The foreign-exchange department was the busiest and most important. More than thirty transactions were carried out on a daily basis and it was vital that a replacement for the main dealer be found as soon as possible. He had been in his job for many years and some considered him virtually irreplaceable.

The boy, while pressing on with his humdrum duties, was nevertheless monitoring everything that went on in the department. He felt confident that the day would come when he would be able to deal successfully himself. His powers of observation and his capacity to absorb knowledge at a rapid rate were going to stand him in good stead when the time came. But he also knew, in terms of the traditional culture of the bank, that it was too soon to aspire to the status of dealer. He did not dare to think such a thing might happen. Fate would have to start turning the accepted realities topsy-turvy first.

Nevertheless, it occurred to him, the manager's philosophy in assessing the candidate for any particular job had always had an eccentric edge to it. The boy recalled how he had been recruited to the bank in the first place, against all reason, when he asserted that he would never be able to differentiate a debit from a credit and had always regarded banking as a boring occupation. Might something similar happen again? Might he be asked to take on a job that he had never been trained for? Admittedly he had been part of the foreign-exchange department for more than a year by now, and so he must have a comprehensive knowledge of its workings that few others on the horizon could have matched. These thoughts helped to reassure him amid all his doubts.

The replacement for the main dealer became a major topic of speculation among the other employees. There was no one in the bank who was capable of filling his shoes in the opinion of most of them. The only solution had to be to recruit someone from outside. As all this uncertainty continued, the crucial call came like a thunderbolt when it was least expected. The boy was summoned to the office of the manager, who began the conversation by informing the boy officially that the foreign-exchange dealer was seriously ill and was unlikely to return. The bank was therefore actively seeking a replacement. Was the boy happy working in that department, he went on to ask; did he see a future for himself in the bank generally? This time the boy was very positive in his answers. He even dared to hint that he would like to be considered for the vacant position. It was a bold statement that carried a slight tinge of arrogance, and it could easily have misfired. To the boy's amazement, the manager never blinked. He braced himself for whatever might follow as the manager paused, then began to speak again:

'For the past year I've kept a close eye on you. I've noted changes. They've been for the better in attitude and discipline. This is very encouraging for the bank, and in my judgement the time has come when we ought to give your career a boost. We look to reap long-term benefits in the opportunities we offer employees. In return for their loyalty to the bank we give them the security of a lifelong career. How does that sound to you?'

In the 1950s, a job for life was still something to strive for. The manager's words were like music to the boy's ears. He could hardly believe his good fortune. It was clear he was about to be offered the prize job; that it was his for the taking. On his journey home, the mounting sense of excitement set his head spinning. That night he hardly slept. As the reality of the situation started to dawn, all sorts of apprehensive questions began to run through his mind. Was he being over-confident: landing himself, out of sheer bravado, in a corner from which he could only extricate himself at great cost? The ball was now rolling, and if he backed down and opted for a less hazardous appointment, he was going to be virtually finished and somehow disgraced. Future ambitions would be badly impaired if not irretrievably damaged. It had been the same every time he changed schools as a boy: always he had agonized over every move and was a bundle of nerves till he settled into the new situation and realized the panic had been quite unnecessary, even foolish. He now invoked these memories of the past, persuading himself that he could take up the offered challenge and meet it standing on his head. Finally, in the early hours of the morning, sleep overtook him.

He left for work next day with his cockiness renewed, ready to accept the job and throw himself into all that it entailed. The months that followed were his proving ground. He learnt fast whatever was expected of him. On the one hand, he showed himself able to live up to the pressures; on the other, he found he was being acknowledged by the foreign-exchange fraternity as someone of exceptional ability and a market leader. In the world of dealing you were only as good as your last success: it was an iron rule that kept you constantly on your toes. The bank's central dictum was that you were employed to make money for the company and its clients. You could achieve this aim on a daily basis, yet never receive a word of congratulation. It was what you were paid for; what was expected of you. Your expertise and efforts were integral to the way the whole system operated. One day's loss, however minimal or insignificant, led to brickbats. No context for the loss would be taken into account. It was a matter of being summoned to the manager's office to be hauled over the coals. No excuses or explanations were acceptable. The sin of making a loss was neither tolerable nor forgivable. It was, as it will always remain, the very basis of capitalism, though the fact is never openly admitted.

In Royal Crescent, life for the boy and Maria changed little as a result of these new challenges, except that he became too exhausted during the week to pursue any active social agenda. Instead they spent quiet evenings at home. They had acquired a small television set and watched programmes that were still all in black and white. The set was kept in the bedroom, which had an exceptionally large bed. It occupied almost the entire space, leaving only a narrow passage on one side to give access to the bed itself. The bed was to gain a certain notoriety for various reasons. First and foremost, it became the social centre on which visitors reclined to converse or to watch such series as *Rawhide*, starring a young Clint Eastwood. Later on it became a refuge where women friends, bizarre as it may seem, could take shelter if they were homeless or sick. But therein lies another tale perhaps destined for future telling.

The boy was undergoing a significant transformation at work. Dealing with the hard, uncompromising realities of money was making him into a man. His mushrooming into manhood happened with such speed that he appeared to be overtaking himself. His entire attitude to life began to change beyond recognition as his boyhood world shrank until it occupied no more than a narrow particle in the infinity of time. The transitional passage of boy into man marked the start of something completely new. It was as if little in all his past had ever existed. No chronicle of those years had been written down, and the memories of them he had in his head were something he unconsciously packed away. He could not know that he was entering a period of respite before heartbreak and glory would together engulf him.

While the life of a foreign-exchange dealer was hectic, it was also liberating in many ways. He felt that he was growing to fill the space within himself. His confidence grew as he realized how the pressures of the job were the salvation for which he had been searching subconsciously. His subservience faded away, at least when he was on the phone in the midst of dealing transactions. The notion of power was entering into his bloodstream, if only momentarily. A deal, once it was done, was not to be undone, so real unchallengeable power was vested in him in that sense. While he remained very much answerable to his masters, the decision he took at a moment of transaction was always the overriding factor. The experience began to shape his character and personality in ways that would reach forward into the years to come, when he found himself in a position to wield power and authority on his own behalf.

The financial-transaction department in the bank was a tough school in which to learn these lessons. It made him more and more determined to excel in this field that had not been his choice. He began to like and appreciate it for the contribution it promised to make to his future, wherever it lay. Another major change was imminent. It was heralded a few months later by a telephone call from a well-known Palestinian banker, Yusif Bedas. A new adventure was on the horizon; it would enable him to get back in touch with his roots after a hiatus of ten years, involving events as fascinating and bizarre as any he had previously known. The boy became a man. He had begun to assume his own identity and was no longer referred to as the boy. Instead, from now on, he would be known as Naim Attallah, who as a young boy had come from Nazareth.